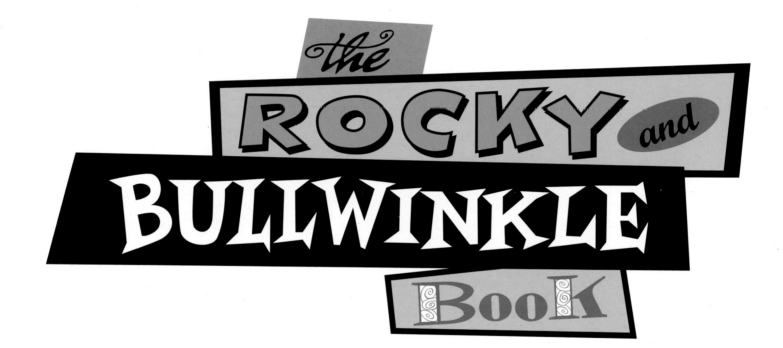

The ROCKY and BULLWINKLE Book

BY LOUIS CHUNOVIC

BANTAM BOOKS

New York   Toronto   London   *Frostbite Falls   Sydney   Auckland

THE ROCKY AND BULLWINKLE BOOK
A Bantam Book / November 1996

Copyright © 1996 by Ward Productions, Inc. All rights reserved.
Licensed by MCA Publishing Rights, a Division of MCA, Inc.

Creative Concept Direction by John Hornick.
Commissioned Photography by Bill Nation.
Design and Production by Axiom Design.

Library of Congress Catalog Card Number: 96-84876.

ISBN 0-553-10503-5

Published simultaneously in the United States and Canada

Bantam Books are published by Bantam Books, a division of Bantam
Doubleday Dell Publishing Group, Inc. Its trademark, consisting of the
words "Bantam Books" and the portrayal of a rooster, is Registered
in U.S. Patent and Trademark Office and in other countries. Marca
Registrada. Bantam Books, 1540 Broadway, New York, New York, 10036.

PRINTED IN CHINA

TOP   10 9 8 7 6 5 4 3 2 1

DEDICATION

For the Next
Generation &
in particular
Amber Ward &
Nina Carolyn
Scott Misch &
Lucia Nicoletta
Scott Misch

CONTENTS

ACKNOWLEDGEMENTS

My thanks to Ramona Ward and Tiffany Ward, Carey and Ron Ward, Carol Stevens, Ron Stark, Michael Silverman, Victoria Scott, Nancy Cushing-Jones, Bill Hurtz, John Hornick, Linda Simmons Hayward, Chris Hayward, Matt Groening, June Foray, Dr. Michael A. Feiler, Jep Epstein, Jim Critchfield, Skip Craig, William Conrad, Paul Clinton, Allan Burns, Howard Brandy, Yardena Arar. Their help made this book possible. ☞

Appreciation, too, for the people who made the magic: The following persons wrote, directed, animated, incarnated, produced, or made other antihistamine contributions to Rocky and His Friends and The Bullwinkle Show:

VOICE ACTORS

June Foray (Rocket J. Squirrel, Natasha Fatale, Nell Fenwick)

Paul Frees (Boris Badenov and Inspector Fenwick)

William Conrad (Narrator)

Edward Everett Horton (Narrator, "Fractured Fairy Tales")

Hans Conried (Snidely Whiplash)

Bill Scott (Bullwinkle J. Moose, Dudley Do-Right, Mister Peabody)

Walter Tetley (Sherman)

Charles Ruggles (Aesop)

Daws Butler (Aesop's son)

DIRECTORS

Bill Hurtz

Pete Burness

Ted Parmelee

Lew Keller

Sal Faillace

Gerard Baldwin

George Singer

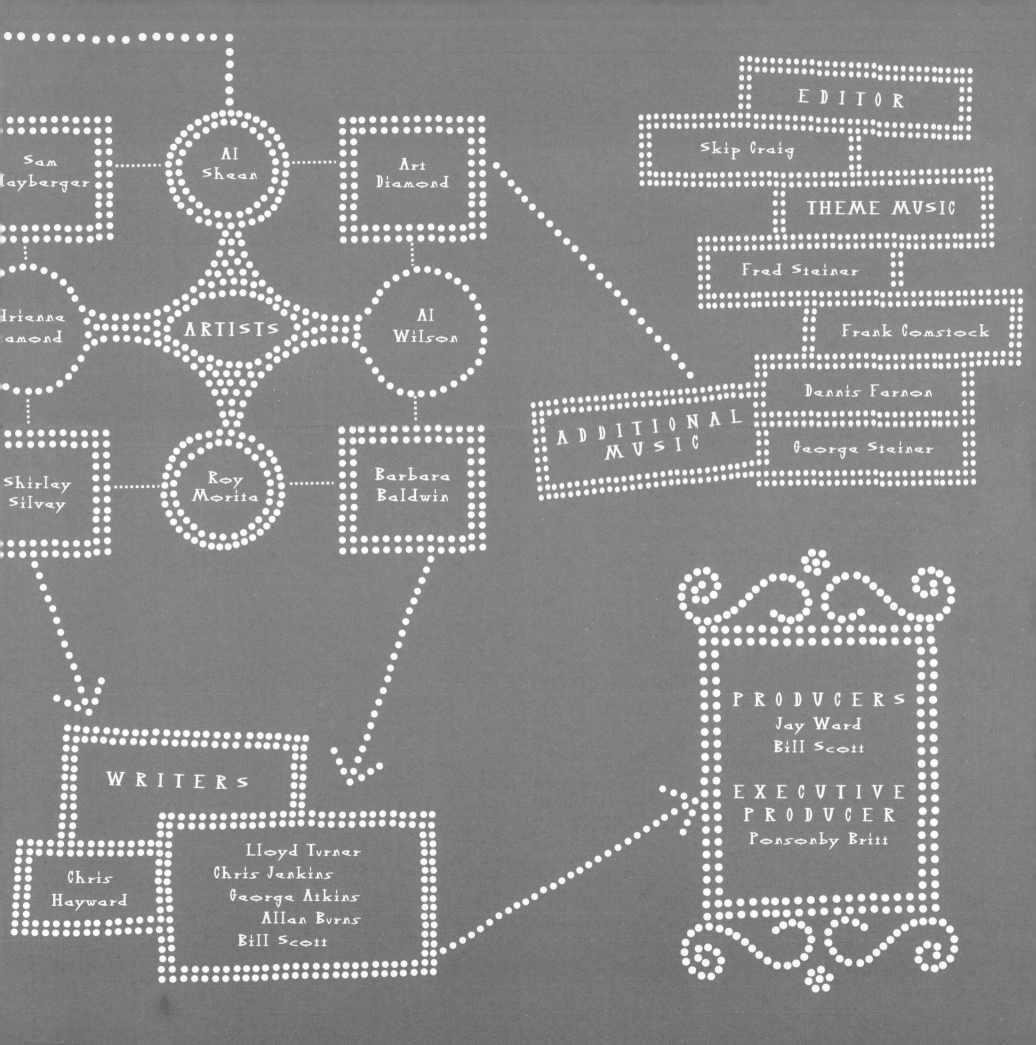

PLUDES & BRIFFETS

personal biography of Rocket J. Squirrel

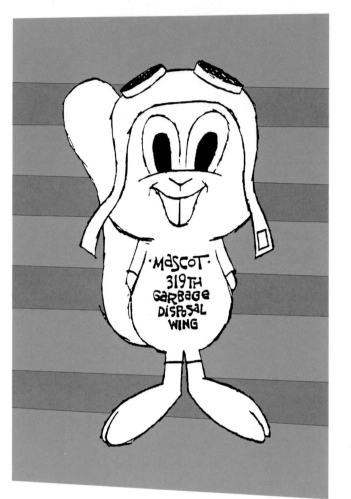

(For additional copies of this biography, hand-printed on heavy parchment and illuminated by Benedictine monks, send $100 in coin to: Jay Ward Productions, Hollywood, California.)

Rocky the Flying Squirrel, is, in addition to being the lifelong friend of Bullwinkle Moose's, the proud mascot of the Air Force 319th Garbage Disposal and Sanitation Wing. With Bullwinkle, he is one-half of a team that is fearless, stainless, and brainless.

Educated in private schools (squirrels were not yet integrated), Rocky majored in snare drums at Juilliard (he was indeed the school's first drum major) before finishing up at Cal Tech (Calvin's School of Supermarket Technology).

Despite his obvious sophistication, Rocky still retains his squirrel's penchant for collecting nuts, as witness his partner, Bullwinkle.

In his crusade against evil, Rocky has exhibited one of the most remarkable demonstrations of obtuseness in history, being flim-flammed and conned by even the most transparent rascals he comes in contact with. Yet, it is this same Rocket J. Squirrel who carries on a personal correspondence with Dr. Albert Schweitzer. (Dr. Schweitzer is a veterinary dentist in Tarzana, California.)

Little wonder, then, why Rocky's portrait (tastefully executed in bottle caps and colored chicken feathers) occupies a prominent place in the Farmers' and Swineherds' National Bank in his hometown of Frostbite Falls, Minnesota.

personal biography of Bullwinkle J. Moose

(A handy reference for writers, students, TV columnists, fan clubs, scandal magazines, and collectors of trivia. Also useful for lining garbage pails and wrapping sandwiches.)

The star of *The Bullwinkle Show* is more than just a moose. He is the finest example of the great North American clod. Having been born and raised in Frostbite Falls, Minnesota, he attended the Philpott School for Exceptional Children (he was the only student with antlers, which *would* tend to make him exceptional) and M.I.T. (the Moose Institute of Toe-dancing).

After distinguished service in the armed forces as a destroyer radar mast and an officers' club hatrack, Bullwinkle decided to study acting under the great student of Stanislavski's, Francis the Talking Horse.
Early in his training, Bullwinkle was alternately determined to become an animated duck, a bunny rabbit, and an iguana, but a singular lack of interest by casting directors persuaded him to abandon this approach.
After several off-Broadway roles (in Laos and Yucca Flats, Nevada), Bullwinkle hit the Great White Way in *Irma la Moose* and *Charley's Antlers.* (The Great White Way, incidentally, is the main street of Frostbite Falls, which is snowed in eleven months of the year.)

Away from the Jay Ward Productions Studio (where *The Bullwinkle Show* is filmed and decontaminated), Bullwinkle likes nothing better than curling up in front of a fire with a pile of good books. "They burn so nice and slow," he says.

Part of Bullwinkle's success has been due to his animal intelligence. "He has more brains in his little finger," says Producer Ward, "than he has in his whole head!"

personal biography of Boris Badenov

(Excellent for inducing bad dreams and frightening disobedient children.)

BoRiS BadeNov ™

The resident villain of *The Bullwinkle Show* bills himself as "The World's Greatest No-Goodnik" and so far no one has stepped up to challenge this claim. His past is mostly shrouded in mystery, although it is fairly certain that he was reared in Pottsylvania, a country whose entire population is made up of spies, secret agents, and saboteurs. (The Pottsylvania *Eavesdropper* is the world's only newspaper printed in invisible ink.) A fun-loving youngster, fond of tying cats' tails to car bumpers, Boris learned his ABCs (Arson, Bomb-throwing, and Conspiracy) in Pottsylvanian public schools before being offered a scoundrelship to U.S.C. (The University of Safe-cracking). He graduated magna cum louse, mainly on the strength of his heinous contributions to his fraternity's Hell Week stunts. He is remarkably durable, having fallen off 26 cliffs in speeding cars, having been blown up at least 14 times (mostly with his own bombs), and having the following objects dropped on his head: 98 flowerpots, 2 safes, innumerable boulders, an Edsel, and his female conspirator, Natasha. When asked to comment on his secret of durability, he generally shrugs and mutters "Vic Tanski." Little is known of his relationship with Natasha, but it is assumed to be unsavory. In his leisure moments, Boris can be found puttering in his garden of Venus's-flytraps, walking his Gila monster, or working on his *Fireside Crook Book*. A member of the Van Gogh Society, he also collects ears.

HISS!

BOO!

personal biography of Natasha Fatale

MISS TRANSYLVANIA

Natasha Fatale, feminine counterpart of Boris Badenov, is a former Miss Transylvania. Although most of her younger life remains a mystery, there is substantial evidence that Natasha is the only child of Axis Sally and Count Dracula. Expelled from college for instigating sit-in demonstrations at a local cemetery, she became an apprentice witch but unfortunately "washed out" in flight school. At this point Natasha, then nineteen, packed her earthly belongings in a voodoo bag and sailed for the New World on the Italian freighter *Lucrezia Borgia*, which had on earlier trips introduced the Japanese beetle, typhus, and Lucky Luciano to our shores. For two years she worked at odd jobs in and around New York – modeling for Charles Addams, popping out of cakes at embalmers' stag parties. Her association with Boris was first noted in 1948, when they were both booked for hurling rocks at Girl Scout cookie sellers. Natasha has been wearing Boris's pin (in her nose) ever since. Although Boris has repeatedly asked for her hand, she has adamantly refused to part with it. Away from the set of *The Bullwinkle Show,* Natasha raises tarantulas and is active in civic affairs, being national chairman of the Society to Restore the Real Meaning of Halloween.

"Well, Junie, looks like we've corrupted another generation," says Bill Scott, the affable voice of a certain famous cartoon moose, one fine day sometime in the early 1980s to June Foray, the pixieish woman who doesn't so much sound like Rocket J. Squirrel as she seems to channel him.

Indeed they have, as they continue to do to this very day. The original generation of Rocky and Bullwinkle fans includes such Boomer luminaries as filmmaker Steven Spielberg, actress Whoopi Goldberg, and science-fiction writer Ray Bradbury, but surely their number-one fan is Matt Groening, creator of The Simpsons.

The production offices for *The Simpsons* are in two nondescript buildings in an out-of-the-way oasis, shaded and green, on the Twentieth Century Fox Studios lot near Century City in Los Angeles. Groening's own office is cluttered and informal, with enough Simpsons merchandising and paraphernalia scattered about to stock a fair-sized Bart Boutique.

Groening himself, Hollywood's best-known cartoonist, is a shaggy-haired, laid-back baby boomer whose latest toy is an Apple PowerBook.

Like his professional hero, Jay Ward, the presiding genius behind Rocky and Bullwinkle, he laughs easily and often; unlike the legendary recluse, he's easy to talk to and comfortable around the press.

Let's talk about Rocky and Bullwinkle. How much of an influence was Jay Ward on your life?

Well, the thing I liked about Rocky and Bullwinkle the most is that it was the only cartoon that my parents would actually sit down and watch with the kids. And they laughed at the jokes, they laughed at the jokes that I didn't get – Kerward Derby and all those puns – and it was just such a thrill, you know, to have a boring old grown-up appreciate the medium of animation, which, as all kids know, is the most magical, wonderful thing in the world.

I was fascinated by the minimal animation, and the sloppiness, that it could be so good. I thought about it a lot and came to the realization the animation doesn't matter that much. It's good writing, good voices, good music that made Rocky and Bullwinkle so much fun to watch.

In fact, it was those shows that encouraged me to go into animation myself. From watching that show when I was a kid, it was one of my fantasies to grow up and have my own cartoon show. It was a *big* influence.

Do you have kids now? Mm-hmm.

Do they watch?

They've watched a few episodes. They're pretty young. One's two and one's four. [But] they like the beginning, when Rocky's flying around. They like all that stuff.

Is the Rocky and Bullwinkle animation style more of an influence on *Life in Hell,* your minimalist newspaper comic, than on *The Simpsons?*

There's a simplicity in the drawing that definitely I picked up on. There's also a crudity to the design – heh-heh – that I found really, um, inviting. A lot of cartoon art in both print and animation is intimidating in its mysteriousness. You can't figure out how it was done, and Rocky and Bullwinkle seemed almost like, you know, doodles come to life. I liked that as well.

The voices were great. June Foray [the voice of both Rocket J. Squirrel and Natasha Fatale], Bill Scott [the voice of Bullwinkle, Peabody, and Dudley Do-Right] and the others – they had fantastic voices.

It served an educational purpose as well, because – heh-heh – that's where I got my first doses of fairy tales, and unfortunately – hah-hah! – where I got a lot of history. From Mister Peabody! Hah! Hah-hah-hah-hah!

I know you once said you were trying to do an episode where Homer and Bart are home **watching the Thanksgiving Day parade, and they see the Bullwinkle balloon.**

Did you do that? Mm-hmm.

Yeah. I think legally we couldn't actually show Bullwinkle, [so] I think we showed the antler of a moose.

Could've been the *Northern Exposure* moose. Hah-hah-hah-hah-*hah!* Imagine what you will!

The antler of a giant inflated moose! Who else could it be?

Any other references in the show?

Well, there's Homer J. Simpson and Bartholomew J. Simpson, named after Rocket J. Squirrel and Bullwinkle J. Moose.

You know, we had June Foray on the show, on the very first episode. She played a woman who ran a baby-sitting service and [also] a happy little elf in a cartoon show that Bart and Lisa were watching. Her voice was so distinctive, it so recalled all her brilliant cartoon work that it stuck out, 'cause we were trying to get away from reminding people that [The Simpsons] was a cartoon.

I worship her, she's SOOO fantastic.

So, did you have to cut her out of the first episode?

Oh, no-no-no. We used her. It was just that it was *sooo* associated with a certain sound....We did not use any of the great cartoon voice actors because we were trying to do something different, although it was a joy to work with her.

You know the great promotions for Rocky and Bullwinkle? **The parades, the picnic at the Plaza hotel,** that sort of thing? **You don't do any of that for** The Simpsons, do you?

No. Well, the only thing we did – it's not even similar – is have a giant inflatable Bart in the Macy's [Thanksgiving] parade....

You told me on the phone that you thought you met Jay Ward once.

Well, I think I did, I think I did. Back when we were working on *The Simpsons* when it was on *The Tracey Ullman Show*…I drove by the Dudley Do-Right Emporium, saw that it was open and said, "Ah-hah, I'll get all my Christmas shopping done," and I went in there and I bought a whole bunch of Rocky and Bullwinkle items, memorabilia, and I bought a lot of cassette tapes of the music from the show.

I believe the man behind the counter was Jay Ward.

What did he look like?

White hair, as I recall, a big white moustache. Is that Jay Ward?

Sounds like Jay Ward, except his wife says the hair was always brown.

He reminded me of Captain Crunch, okay?…So, anyway, I started complimenting him about how brilliant all these things were, and he got very shy, and he had a shy smile, and he started to back away. Hee - hee - hee. So I thought, "Yup, that must be Jay Ward," and I went back to the animation studio and gave all these presents out.

What did you tell him? Do you remember?

Well, I just told him how brilliant I thought the show was....The writing, the music, and the voices were all unmatched, and it was such a great collaboration of those three things.

You were a fan of the animation style too, weren't you, even though it was kind of, ah –

It does what it does really well. There's no unnecessary movement, there's extremely quick cutting, I love the voice-overs, the narration, and I love the use of the [same] animation again and again.

You mean –

In our last episode, we saw – hah - hah - hah - hah! And also, by the way, there *was* some suspense, some real suspense. The giant mechanical-munching mice – what were those called?

The metal-munching moon mice.

Hah! I loved that! I saw it again, I guess it was in college, and [originally] I thought, "Oh, I get all these jokes," so now I'm watching it again and I think, "Uh, oh! Waitaminute! Now there's a whole nother level of joke that I can get!"

Do you have a favorite joke?

Ummm…

I do. I don't remember the circumstances, but there's this newt, this little frog, on the stairs, and someone says, "Look, there's a newt descending a staircase." Hah-hah-**hah!**

The joke that occurs to me is just a reference to the Kerward Derby, only

because I heard that it irritated [the real] Durward Kirby so much.

He threatened to sue.

Hah! To me, that's one of things that any cartoonist craves; it's what I call the Elmer Fudd syndrome. When somebody behaves like Elmer Fudd – hah! – you know, that makes **you** Daffy Duck!

Rocky and Bullwinkle **are quite well aware of being cartoon characters on a TV show, and**

they're always talking back to the Narrator. They're like English music-hall actors wearing these costumes. Any of that in The Simpsons?

I guess we consciously decided to go the other way and have the Simpsons not aware of themselves as cartoon characters or as celebrities. We have toyed with it: What would happen if you were a normal American family sitting at home and [then-President] George Bush said that Americans should be more like the Waltons than the Simpsons? We did animate Homer watching it and going "Oh?" – hah-**hah.** And Bart says, "Hey, man, we're just like the Waltons. Both families are praying for an end to the Depression!"

Hah-hah! Anything else you wanna say about the Moose and the Squirrel?

Umm, you know, just in thinking about how you keep people's attention with the same animation over and over again: that one repeated sequence in the show where Rocky and Bullwinkle are running back and forth and they get struck by lightning and they go down under the earth and they come up with the flowers. That, I **love** it, I've never gotten tired of it!…I still don't understand the logic of it, but I love it.

Yeah, I like the opening too where Rocky's diving down and Bullwinkle's running around below with a tub of water.

Yeah. This is another thing I've gotten from Rocky and Bullwinkle: Rocky and Bullwinkle was a cartoon that rewarded you for paying attention. Very *very* little of what's on television rewards you for paying attention. The closer you look, the more you see the holes, the sloughing off. But with Rocky and Bullwinkle, if you're watching carefully, there're lots of extra jokes in there. It's something that I've tried to do myself.

AND NOW...

..."Hey, Rocky, watch me pull a rabbit outta the hat."

"Again?!"

"Presto!"

"Rooooar!"

"Oops wrong hat."

They may never have pulled that elusive rabbit from the hat, but, as generations of kids of all ages will attest, that big-hearted north-country Moose and that all-American flying squirrel – along with the memorable likes of an educated beagle and a certain Royal Canadian Mountie – sure do know how to make the magic.

The formula: witty dialogue, self-aware characters (in a cartoon yet!), shameless show-biz shtik, and a fearless way with the cultural icons of the times, as well as with the timeless platitudes that are with us yet.

Take for example *The Frostbite Falls Picayune Intelligence,* Rocky and Bullwinkle's hometown newspaper (circulation: 47). It's had the same headline for the past fifteen years: COLD WAR CONTINUES. Remember: In the rest of the world, which, rather dumbfounded, was originally watching these adventures on a newfangled home appliance known colloquially as the Tee Vee, it's just 1960 and the cold war *is* in its fifteenth year of deep freeze.

But in Frostbite Falls there are even more modern wonders than that: *Atomic-powered roller skates,* available for just sixteen box tops!

Easily redeemed by one Bullwinkle J. Moose, whose vast box-top collection rests safely at Farmers and Swineherds, the local national bank. Or does it? That two-faced big-nosed fuse lighter from down Pottsylvania way, Boris Badenov, and his slinky sidekick, Natasha Fatale, even now are cooking up a Fiendish Plan, and, doubtless, sooner or later, it'll involve a Pottsylvanian Persuader (two pounds of TNT in a one-pound bag...with a short fuse). After all, dollinks, it isn't for nothing that

Fearless Leader has bestowed on Boris Badenov the highest medal his native land has to offer, namely, the Pottsylvanian Double Cross!

Sure, Rocket J. Squirrel and his big-antlered pal would be only too happy to rest on their many laurels – "When it comes to humility," sez Mister Moose, "I'm the great-est" – and not to be forever saving the world from Pottsylvanian spies, man-eating plants, and scrooch-gun-wielding moon men, tend-ing, instead, their garden (Rocky's partial to raising prize-winning Checkered Begonias). But Natasha Fatale and that Dracula of the cartoon indus-try, Boris Badenov, are perennially raising problems. As Boris sez, "Vee gotta, or vee von't be in the next episode!"

Badenov is, after all, one dastardly villain who knows from whence comes his next residuals check. For example:

When from the top of Sam Hill (which isn't too far from the lovely Veronica Lake and the ever-popular Isle of Lucy) Natasha espies a certain moose: "Boris, is moose you said you killed in previous episode!"

Badenov replies with an elaborate shrug: "It's his show. If he vants to be hard to kill, let him."

In fact, even though Boris is even not  above forcing the Narrator to play a previ-ous episode backwards in order to learn valuable information, no plot is too elaborate and no plan is too fiendish to not take time out to engage in what our ubiquitous Narrator is wont to call

"airy persiflage." And that even goes for the scheme to derail our two heroes in their quest to make Moosylvania the fifty-second state by disguising Butte, Montana, as Washington, D.C., complete with green Frankenstein stat-ue atop the Capitol dome.

A Fiendish Plan, yes, but it's taught the boomers and their offspring a valuable civics lesson: There should not be a green monster atop our national dome.

Not that the Rocky and Bullwinkle show hasn't always been highly educational, mixing entertainment with education as easily as $E = MC^z$.

Thus, when Boris and Natasha abscond from the Kingdom of Normandie (which, as all Los Angelenos know, is near Third and La Brea) with a collection of French Old Masters, the pictures naturally end up as wallpaper in Bullwinkle's chicken coop. And, another time, farther down the river, when the big moose finds himself caught up in an antebellum South affair of honor, he ~~opines,~~ states "I thought 'a duel' meant 'good-bye' in French."

Which causes Boris to more or less reflect: "I'm such a chicken, my favorite composer is Noel Coward."

And if it isn't enough that Rocket J. and Bullwinkle J. deliver what we are now pleased to call "pro-social values" for miles – or, as Bullwinkle

Given the language style of Rocky & Bullwinkle, we allow this mistake of "from whence".
Same here with the double "evens".

OK. That one's too much. "Opine"'s just the wrong word.

declares when listing his qualifications for a movie-theater-usher position: "I been in the dark most of my life" — there are those other merrymakers who share the half hour with our heroes to consider: They *really* mold young minds!

Take Dudley Do-Right, that stalwart Royal Canadian Mountie, he of the square jaw, the true heart, and the pea brain. His stirring north-of-the-border adventures not only educate young minds in the traditional values — duty, honor, love of country and of horse — but he and his archenemy, Snidely Whiplash, embody a noble show-business tradition as well, namely, that of the stage name — Acne Pitts and Dewar Diddy for Dudley, and Madison A. Swill and Chief Running Sore for the nefarious Snidely, with the lovely carrot-haired Nell Fenwick naturally played by none other than Sweetness N. Light.

Whiplash forecloses mortgages, ties innocent young damsels to railroad tracks, and uses foul trickery (such as winning the annual Skagway dogsled-pulling contest with a disguised elephant or breaking out of Elevenworth prison in a submarine) to best the right-doing Dudley. Aiding him betimes is that musical band of villains, the Disloyal Canadians.

But while, somehow, the Mounties continue to get their man (and their occasional monster), the Rocky and Bullwinkle show's skewed morality plays never stop north of the border or south of Moosylvania, or even in the present day. "Aesop and Son," "Fractured Fairy Tales," and "Mister Peabody's Improbable History" all deliver classically cracked education.

Aesop, too, is basically an old trouper, a nasal raconteur with a smarmy lounge-lizard delivery. Kids everywhere know the type: the unctuous school principal raining platitudes down from his Olympian heights on a captive assemblage of students. But this Aesop tells not only the traditional fables ("The Hare and the Tortoise," and so forth), he regales his wise-cracking son with such unlikely fabliaux as "The Frogs and the Beaver," "The Lion and the Aardvark," and "The Jackrabbits and the Mule." And the morals are invariably punning groaners. Consider the

moral that ends the story of Clem and Charley, the two practical-joking desert-prospecting jackrabbits. They take for granted the restauranteur/mule, who serves only water at his one-table establishment, until the day he's no longer to be found: *You never miss the waiter until the water runs dry* is, of course, the lesson there.

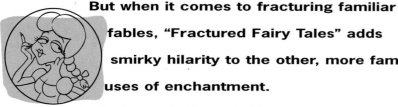 But when it comes to fracturing familiar fables, "Fractured Fairy Tales" adds smirky hilarity to the other, more familiar uses of enchantment.

And why not? Doesn't Mother Frog herself warn her five-eight son, Filbert, who's become enamored of the golden-apple-laden princess living atop a glass mountain, that "it's a frog-eat-frog existence?"

The moral of that story? "It's better to be a big frog in a small pond than a small frog on a glass mountain. Besides, who can eat golden apples?"

Indeed. But when it comes to Sleeping Beauty or Little Red Riding Hood or Goldilocks or Tom Thumb, apparently you can't get too much of a good thing. Time and again these classic fairy tales are fractured and refracted, told and retold.

Not only do we have the story of "Sleeping Beauty," who in this telling isn't really asleep at all, we also get the tale (and the tail) of "Speeding Beauty," who gets turned into a race horse by a wicked witch, as well as the story of "Sweeping Beauty," a rather plain, hardworking lass who's suffering from chronic lack of beauty sleep.

Take Little Red, for another example. In one "Fractured Fairy Tale" she's the proprietor of a Riding Hood Shop and has a customer who wants a wolfskin hood. In another "Fractured" version of the famous fairy tale, the wolf has turned over a new leaf, joining Riding Hoods Anonymous and taking the pledge to swear off his favorite dish ("Though Riding Hoods you may not munch, there's nothing wrong with a Grandma lunch"). And yet another rendition recounts the misadventures of Little *Fred* Riding Hood.

And you can be sure that in the "Fractured" retelling of "Hansel and Gretel," when Hansel leaves the famous trail of bread crumbs in the woods, Gretel is bound to mutter, "That plan is for the birds!"

And then there's the world's smartest talking dog, who does for history what the "Fairy Tales" do for myth and fable. Inventor of the Way-Back Machine, Mister Peabody is a dapper beagle with a nose for newsworthy historical events. Not surprisingly, he has his own boy — wide-eyed, red-haired Sherman, a witness to the most preposterous of historical events.

Remember heroic Lawrence of Arabia? Contriving to assist the pixilated Englishman by putting the sultan and his army into large barns filled with straw, Peabody explains to his boggled boy: "Apparently, Sherman, somebody likes Turkey in the straw."

And Robin Hood, in the Peabody version, takes a tumble: After a bump on the head, what he really wants to do is steal from the poor to give to the rich.

But perhaps Sherman and Peabody's most famous time-traveling adventure of all is the trip way back to the year 1611, when one Will Shakespeare has just finished composing his master work, "Romeo and Zelda." But title trouble aside, what *really* irks the Bard is that darned Francis Bacon!

Upon being bopped on the noggin with a flowerpot by his rival, Shakespeare delivers the immortal line: "Bacon, you'll fry for this!" and later, after getting his revenge, the Greatest Writer in the English Language adds with some satisfaction: "That should settle Bacon's hash!"

No less than the rest of the Rocky and Bullwinkle troupe, the erudite Mister Peabody is astute about the new medium in which he appears. For instance, in the Way-Back version, archer William Tell has lost his spectacles and can't see to shoot the apple off his son's head. But his arrow eventually flies true, with a little help from the magnet that Peabody surreptitiously places in the apple on the hapless boy's head. Still, Mister Peabody is moved to observe that forever after the archer's name will be linked to a major cause of eye trouble: Tell-evision.

"Gee," Rocky sez wonderingly at the end of an adventure after Bullwinkle steps obliviously off a cliff, "an unhappy ending."

Caught by his antlers and dangling from a cliff-face branch, Bullwinkle agrees, "This must be one of them adult cartoons."

Indeed it is, and that it aired originally in the late fifties and early sixties seems almost miraculous in retrospect. How did they do it?

Set the Way-Back Machine for a day in November 1959....

Tinny trumpets sound, cymbals crash; jagged lightning streaks across a surreal sky....
Here they come again, tumbling through the perilous air, only to sprout up beaming among the daisies and sunflowers....
There goes Squirrel, swooping and soaring off the high platform, the very picture of grace and exuberance, while below, Moose galumphs along with a barrel of water....

In 1959, on the cusp of the Kennedy sixties, two years after Sputnik first circled the earth, a cartoonish, beeping wake-up call from the Ruskie Red Menace inaugurating the space age, an all-American flying squirrel and a know-it-all moose took to the airwaves. They remain there to this day.

Television in the fifties was still brand new – you got three, maybe four channels if you were lucky; reception was always iffy – and there were fewer rules. No one knew then what TV animation really looked like, if it was just for kids or could be for adults too, or even what time period it was supposed to be on. (The Saturday morning animation ghetto came later.)

The new, cost-effective "partial" animation style of early TV, as opposed to the expensive "full" animation of theatrical features, put a premium on clever writing and dialogue and on sparkling "voice actors" who could convey character and emotion. It was, in fact, the Jay Ward way of

doing cartoons for television, and to this day it's still the formula for TV animation success.

Improbably, considering that they were the product of a ragtag animation studio best known for what it *wasn't* (not Disney, not Warner, not part of the painterly style of classical animation, and not aimed just at kids), Rocky and Bullwinkle have outlasted their contemporaries – still funny and eminently relevant in the nineties, the Moose and Squirrel are reigning American pop icons, just about as universally known as Marilyn, Elvis, and JFK (or Homer and Bart, for that matter).

An animated series starring Pottsylvanian spy Boris Badenov's perpetually optimistic adversaries, *Mooz and Squirrel,* was, on the face of it, an unlikely oasis of sophisticated satire in the vast wasteland of private eye and cowboy shows that was late-fifties American network TV. And the end of the McCarthyite fifties was not an auspicious time to be stretching the bounds of television humor, as Frostbite Falls's favorite sons blithely did, even tweaking their own network's midbrow pieties. ("What kind of game can you play with *girls?*" Rocky petulantly asks right before the big grudge match between Wossamotta U and the Mud City Manglers' "girls" team. Bullwinkle J. Moose gives the viewer out in TV land a knowing, sidelong look. "Boy," he opines, "this really *is* a children's show." Pausing a beat, he drolly adds, "Parcheesi of course.")

Regularly, they lampooned politicians, bureaucrats, the military, and even the cold war itself. Not that the era wasn't rife with all manner of satirical possibilities.

Consider, for example, dollink, this particular looney historical juxtaposition with its distinctly Boris-and-Natasha feel: In 1959, at a Moscow trade fair in a model suburban kitchen filled with the latest "modern" gadgets, Soviet Premier Nikita "the Shoe Banger" Khrushchev hotly debates the merits of capitalism versus communism with then–Vice President Richard "I Am Not a Crook" Nixon; while later that year, in Southern California, Khrushchev flies into a petulant rage after being denied permission to visit Disneyland. Maybe they could've avoided the Cuban Missile Crisis – or at least the moosle crisis – if they'd taken him to Frostbite Falls, or Moosylvania, instead. At about the same time, *Rocky and His Friends* was debuting on ABC-TV. A pair of three-and-a-half-minute-long breathlessly narrated episodes of Rocky and Bullwinkle's incredible adventures

bookended each half-hour show, beginning with a forty-episode saga about the hunt for mooseberry-powered rocket fuel. The show's final format, however, wasn't fixed until 1961: Between the cliffhanger episodes, "Fractured Fairy Tales" and "Aesop and Son" alternated weekly fables that specialized in twisting traditional parables and delivering ever-more-atrocious puns, while "Mister Peabody's Improbable History," with its intelligent beagle's-eye view of historical events, traded off with that heroically dimbulb, straight-shooting, square-jawed Mountie, Dudley Do-Right. The pixilated prescriptions of "Mister Know-It-All" and the warped rhymes of "Bullwinkle's Corner" completed a mix as powerful as the recipe for Grandma Moose's explosive fudge cake.

Rocky, which in 1961 moved to NBC, where it became *The Bullwinkle Show,* was turned out by a small group of writers and animators mostly working out of the cramped offices of the

Jay Ward Studios on Sunset in Hollywood. What was it like in those late-fifties/early-sixties days?

"It was like the 1930s and the Round Table at the Algonquin," says a writer who was there, "only instead of Hemingway, Parker, and Benchley, there was Jay Ward and his writers and animators…and a moose and a squirrel."

In its heyday the Ward studio was a place, writer Lloyd Turner recalled in a brief and wistful magazine memoir, with an "old-fashioned ice cream and soda fountain, a real popcorn machine just like in the theaters, Sno-Kone and candy machines, jelly beans in a hundred flavors…collections of cigar store Indians and antique barber chairs, and a circus calliope." The product, Turner concluded, of Ward's "eight year-old mind."

Much like Walt Disney, Jay Ward, University of California at Berkely class of '41 and a Harvard MBA, wasn't known as an animator, a writer, or a director. His real title was presiding genius and his real talent was for spotting talent and knowing comedy and for showmanship with an entrepreneurial flair. He knew what he liked (and how to promote it), and what he liked was wildly off beat and pointedly satirical. It also was *never* salacious; after all, although they wrote Rocky to amuse themselves, the writers knew that the children were watching too. In short, as Ward was fond of repeating, the scripts had to be Jay rated.

The eccentric Ward's staff even had a pair of stamps made up: JAY RATED and NOT JAY RATED, his daughter, Tiffany, who grew up in the house the Moose and Squirrel built, recalls. Off-color jokes were never, *ever* Jay rated, she adds brightly, and Jay-rated people had

THE WEEK "ROCKY" DEBUTED ON ABC…

Congressional committees were investigating the TV quiz-show scandals and payola in the music business….

And a page-one headline in *Weekly Variety* warned:

CENSORS HOVERING OVER ALL MEDIA

to be "decent people. They could have a variety of personalities, but they had to be well meaning and, if possible, funny, not personally funny, but have a sense of humor."

People with a sense of humor sought Jay Ward out, perhaps sensing from the unlikely evidence of the TV show that there, on Sunset, was a place where creative work could be as much fun as play, and where magic just might be made.

In many ways, the story of how young Allan Burns found his way to the small studio on Sunset is typical. Today Burns is the multi-Emmy-award-winning writer/producer and co-creator of, among others, *The Mary Tyler Moore Show* and *The Munsters.* Back then he was just a twentysomething kid, a one-time page at NBC Burbank who'd done some cartooning for the *Honolulu Star Bulletin* and was struggling in L.A., burned out on drawing and writing for the crank-it-out greeting-card business. One day he took a break and flipped on the tube.

"I saw this show, *Rocky and His Friends,* and I'd never seen it before, never even heard of it," he recalls. "I was fascinated by what appeared to be a little kids' show in the afternoon, [but] was actually something that made *me* laugh. And this was not something I was accustomed to....

"Here were actual jokes and funny things and satirical stuff going on," he adds, his voice tinged with recollected amazement, "and at the end of these credits that flashed by, I saw the name Jay Ward. I thought, 'I wonder if they're even here in town? It could be New York, it could be anywhere,' But I picked up the phone book and looked up the name Jay Ward and there it was: *Jay Ward Productions, Sunset Boulevard.*"

What young Allan did then is what talented, hungry kids in L.A. have always done and always will do, as they perpetually reenact the great Hollywood Myth:

"I picked up my baggage of several hundred greeting cards that I had done over the years...and I trudged over there and found this weird little building on Sunset, walked in, and there [was] this sort of older woman who [was] harried and [had] difficulty with the switchboard. She just didn't have any time for me at all....

"While I was standing there talking to her, this guy walks in, a guy disguising his baldness with three strips of bacon across his head, [as] someone once described it. This guy was standing there thumbing through mail and...he looks over and says, 'What've you got there?'

and I said, 'It's just some samples from the greeting-card business. Some of it's nice,' not knowing I was talking to Jay Ward....

"Only moments later," Burns continues, "he sort of sits there and looks through this [sample] book and chuckled and chuckled and chuckled. I was very encouraged by the fact that he was chuckling at everything, not knowing he chuckled at stuff he didn't like as well as stuff that he did. I learned that from hard experience later." In fact, Jay's nervous heh-heh-heh was one of his trademark tics, as much a way for this famous recluse and eccentric to keep the unruly world at bay as was the outrageous Gilbert-and-Sullivanesque admiral's costume he often wore on public occasions.

But back then, when he realized that the Perpetual Chuckler was none other than Jay Ward himself, the innocent would-be writer/animator was encouraged. Soon Ward's partner, Bill Scott appeared. Ward and the taller, more gregarious and politically liberal Scott (who was the voice of Bullwinkle, Dudley Do-Right, and Mister Peabody, as well) were Mutt-and-Jeff opposites, but they were both talented and witty and they liked each other, making the contradictions work for them. Scott "kind of grunted his way through the stuff," says Burns. "Then Jay says, 'Yeah, we'll find something for you,' and I said, 'Just like that?' and he said, 'Yeah, well, you're funny, you draw well. I like [your] offbeat stuff. We'll find something. We'll fit you in.'"

And so they did, setting the future award winner to work turning out the copy for a string of hilarious and wildly successful promotional mailers.

Biting the hand that fed him was an integral part of Ward's charm – and probably inevitable, given his staunch sense of aggrieved righteousness when it came to networks and sponsors. But it's precisely that iconoclasm that attracted a razor-sharp group of writers, directors, and animators – some brash newcomers, others veterans of the countless studio wars – to Ward Productions and its gonzo style.

In the hurdy-gurdy credit roll at the end of every Rocky and Bullwinkle show, the executive producer is listed as one "Ponsonby Britt." Actually, there is no such person.

"We had to have an executive producer," Jay Ward told an interviewer some years ago, "but it didn't seem fair that Bill and I were taking all the credit."

"Bill" was Bill Scott, Ward's longtime partner, a big, affable moose of a man who counterpointed the smaller, roly-poly Ward not only physically but politically and temperamentally as well. Scott – the voice of Bullwinkle, Peabody, and Dudley – was the show's head writer and director too. He and Ward comprised an odd couple as unlikely as a, well, as a moose and a flying squirrel.

"Jay was very shy, very inward; Bill was gregarious, a performer, just real outgoing" is how writer Allan Burns remembers it. "They were great friends and they couldn't have disagreed more about politics. Everybody in the place was pretty liberal except Jay, but he would never impose his politics on anybody; it would never occur to him to do that."

"Bill…was always drawing these little cartoons. He loved to draw Jay. The office would be littered with little cartoons."

There was a *Missus Bullwinkle* too, but like exec producer, Ponsonby Britt, she didn't exist either.

Missus Bullwinkle was how then-teenage Linda Simmons signed the twenty to a hundred or so Bullwinkle fan letters she answered every week. One of the animators helped her with the signature, teaching her to make the "B" so that it looked like Bullwinkle's head.

"I was the person who answered the phones, and I answered all the fan mail for Bullwinkle and I did all the press clippings. Every great while, Jay would try to dictate a letter, and I remember so well, in those days I had no idea how to take shorthand…I was so bad at it, when I brought him [a letter] to sign, he'd just start laughing, because who knows what I had put in there…He'd say, 'Send the letter out just like that.'"

Seemingly, though, everything worked out. She learned shorthand and pitched in on the elaborate promotional stunts – helping to organize, for example, the Exotic Dancers League Awards lunch at the Bel-Air Hotel – and sending out the wacky gifts Jay was notorious for giving – just where *do* you put a six-foot-high stuffed gorilla, or a Goodyear tire done up like a Christmas wreath?

Working at Jay Ward Productions on Sunset, Linda Simmons met Chris Hayward, one of the writers. She married him and, with Allan Burns, he went on to create *The Munsters*.

Shy, reclusive Jay Ward cultivated an outlandish public image. But his well-known love of candy and circus calliopes, his walrus mustache and the cartoon admiral's costume, weren't simply PR touches dreamed up by a clever public relations man. Jay Ward was a genuine eccentric and, if you doubt it, listen to his daughter describe her Beverly Hills wedding: "Dad said, 'You're not really my daughter if you don't want to have a fun wedding.' I was twenty-one and I was looking for the fairy tale wedding, *not* the humorous one….He wanted to know if he could have popcorn vendors and monkeys with organ grinders inside the church with trumpeters and all. And of course the church said, 'Are you kidding? No way!'"

But her father, a persistent man, wasn't to be dissuaded. "The surprises started happening afterwards. When we came out, he'd arranged for a 1920s Silver Cloud to drive us between the church and the country club

YOU'VE GIVEN ME THE CONFIDENCE TO GO FORWARD!

[where the reception was held]. As we were driving, there were skywriters that said: *Congratulations Tiffany and Pete.*" When they got to the posh Riviera Country Club, there was the traditional receiving line for the bride and groom and their parents, only... Jay Ward had had a department store dummy dressed up to look just like him, in tails and tennis shoes. And inside the dummy was a tape recorder playing one-liners. "So the dummy stood next to me in the receiving line. People would come [through the line] several times just to hear more of the tape. Nobody paid any attention to the bride." And here's some of what the five hundred guests heard:

Hi, I'm Jay Ward.

Heh-heh-heh....

Drink up! We've only got the hall until five-thirty.

Shove right along there, keep moving, please.

Hi, I'm Jay Ward.

Heh-heh-heh....

Yes, that's right, I do look slimmer in person.

Hi, I'm Jay Ward.

Do you know how to spell "bankrupt"?

Heh-heh-heh....

Would you like to buy a half-hour cartoon series?

Keep it moving, please.

Hi, I'm Jay Ward.

Heh-heh-heh....

You don't suppose you could find a place in your company for the boy Tiff married? Heh-heh-heh....

Hi, I'm Jay Ward....

How'd you like the skywriting? Everything in quiet good taste, I always say.

Hi, I'm Jay Ward. The person standing next to me is a dummy. Heh-heh-heh....

Move along! Move along!

Whaddya mean, this is ridiculous?

Hi, I'm Jay Ward.

Gee, you've put a little weight on, didn't you?

Hah-hah-hah!

Hi, I'm Jay Ward.

My daughter only met this guy last month. Do you know anything about him?

Move along...

You're Amelia Earhart? We've been looking for you. Fly on down the line.

Hi, I'm Jay Ward. Better not eat any of the food, it's all leftovers.

Hi, I'm Jay Ward. Whaddya think of the music? It oughta be good, it's costing me four hundred a song! Heh-heh-heh....

Step lively! Move along. Tighten the line there. And so it went. *Heh-heh-heh.*

June Foray – vivacious, twinkly, and apple-cheeked – is probably the best-known voice actress in all of Hollywood. Hers is the instantly recognizable, chipper, and endlessly optimistic voice of Rocket J. Squirrel himself, as well as of – Hokey smoke! – both slinky Natasha Fatale and stout-hearted Nell Fenwick, Dudley Do-Right's carrot-headed one true love.

June was a little dubious when her agent told her about Rocky, but then she met Jay – "an affable guy who was laughing all the time" – over a two-martini lunch.

"We had one martini, and then two martinis, and then by the end of the lunch he was so affable and his idea was kinda cute, and I was accessible by that point for anything...An idea for a show about a squirrel and a moose sounded just fine."

After about an hour's work on the pilot for *Rocky and His Friends,* an entire year went by. She resumed her busy professional life. (Foray was then, as she continues to be now, much in demand as a voice actress. Among her multitude of credits: raspy-voiced,

WHO WERE THESE UPSTART PRODUCERS, TWEAKING A MIGHTY BROADCAST NETWORK?...

For immediate release
Jay Ward and Bill Scott, creators of "Rocky and his Friends" are here seen hard at work on their latest episode

bobby-pin-flinging Witch Hazel, and Granny, who's always admonishing Sylvester about Tweety.) Finally, one day, her agent called: that squirrel-and-moose show was a go.

For almost four years there were weekly recording sessions, usually in the late afternoon or evening. "It was like going to a picnic every night," enthuses the tiny blond pixie who sounds just like Rocket J. Squirrel. "Jay was always laughing and the actors were always making jokes and ragging on each other."

The Granny and Witch Hazel voices were particular Jay Ward favorites. He was always saying to Foray, "Do the Brooklyn, do the Brooklyn," and for all those fairy godmothers in "Fractured Fairy Tales," it was, "Do the Marjorie Main." As for Rocky, "Jay wanted an all-American boy with a derring-do voice, just caricatured a little bit," she says. So that's what I did. He's got a boy's voice but an adult mind."

And for Natasha, there was always the cold war concern that she not sound too Russian – "They came from Pottsylvania, dollink, so (Jay) wanted a Mideast accent."

They were a singularly eccentric lot, these Wardsters, led by a singularly eccentric man.

THE WRITERS ALL AGREED: YOU HAD TO BE COMMITTED TO WORK FOR JAY WARD....

WHAT'S A JAY WARD?

IT'S A WARD THEY KEEP THE LOONIES IN.

Ward himself thought nothing of gathering up his cronies from the studio for an afternoon at the track, where they could cheer on Thoroughbreds racing under the yellow and orange Bullwinkle colors (even the great Willie Shoemaker rode for the Ward stable at one time; on his back, the stable's insignia: big-antler'd Bullwinkle, of course), or of shutting down the studio, packing the gang into a car, and heading for an impromptu golfing vacation in Phoenix. "One time he had knickers made for all the players," says Ramona Ward with a laugh. And there there was the Great Moustache Growing Contest.

At that time, she recalls, "there were so many hippies around, all up and down Sunset. And Jay says, 'If you can't fight the hippies, join them,' so then they had the moustache-growing contest with a prize for the best." The winner got a trip to Hawaii, and Ward himself grew the walrus moustache that became his trademark.

Working at Ward Productions was "all perks and no salary," as Burns put it. "You ate lavishly and had wonderful times, but there was no money." He remembers sitting morosely in his badly lighted cubicle

IF PRODUCING ROCKY AND BULLWINKLE WAS LIKE GOING TO THE CIRCUS, THEN JAY WARD WAS THE RINGMASTER....

BUT, SURELY, MR. WARD, AS A RESPONSIBLE, ADULT CITIZEN, YOU... OH, FORGET IT!

one day, bemoaning his fate – "I'm twenty-seven years old and writing for a damn moose!" – when Bill Scott fairly bounded in to quip, "Hell, I'm fifty, and I *am* a damn moose."

Ward Productions itself was more like a daffy and decrepit clubhouse for a gang of overaged Lost Boys than the precisely tuned machine that is the typical Hollywood dream factory. Framed posters for obscure movies adorned the walls of Ward's office, which was dominated by cigar store Indians, a circus calliope, and a huge wooden, throne-like chair. Writers often worked in gloomy and dank basement cubicles. For a time the offices were managed by a sullen secretary who spent much of her work time knitting, and whom Ward gleefully refused to fire despite protests from the writers, who felt abused by her unfriendly attitude. In fact, so amused was he by the secretary's antipathy that after a particularly vociferous complaint, he gave her a raise.

The look of the place, says Burns, was like the old joke: "If the termites ever stop holding hands, it will come down." Lunch was martini time, although Ward himself was a teetotaler, Burns recalls, and after, "there was a certain smell in the air that said a lot of naps, and then they'd get back to work."

Wandering the halls were such figures as the debonair and dapper Paul Frees (the voice of Boris), a well-known fifties-era TV announcer, and also the voice of philanthropic John Beresford Tipton in TV's *The Millionaire;* Peter Burness, an Academy Award–winning animation director (for UPA's *Mr. Magoo*); one-armed writer Lloyd Turner – he enjoyed startling visitors by

BAD NEWS, MR. WARD.— YOUR SUGAR SHOWS TRACES OF BLOOD!

sticking pins into his prosthesis — who became a writer, he often said, after starting out as an animator because he kept noticing that the writers were having a good time, laughing while they worked, and who went on to a distinguished TV writing career that included *All in the Family, Maude,* and *Mork and Mindy;* Chris Hayward, another writer, who with Burns went on to create *The Munsters* and *The Smothers Brothers Show;* Burns himself, who with James L. Brooks later co-created such TV series as *The Mary Tyler Moore Show, Rhoda,* and *Lou Grant,* and who was so affected by his early experiences as a Wardster that he fictionized the Jay-rated world in a mid-eighties NBC sitcom called *The Duck Factory,* which starred then-unknown Jim Carrey, who went on to become Ace Ventura, and such veteran character actors as Hans Conried, Charles Ruggles, Edward Everett Horton, and William Conrad. The latter would go on to TV fame as Cannon, but back then he was already well known as a distinctive radio voice. Of those long-ago days Conrad said with real feeling, "It was the most enjoyable show I ever did in my life."

What made those recording sessions so special? Reading the sparkling dialogue was just plain fun, for one thing, and Ward knew that *speed* was one secret of comedy, so he was always urging the voice actors, particularly Conrad, to go "faster, faster, faster." Then there was the affectionate razzing and the cutting cross talk that often reduced June Foray, in particular, to throaty laughs and disbelieving exclamations — "Oh, no-no-no-no," gasped out between giggles, after, say, Bill Scott in his deadpan Bullwinkle voice urged William Conrad to "get larger Jockey shorts" so he could narrate faster, or Paul Frees, with great apparent sincerity, suggested that "Bill [Scott], I think, should represent us at the United Nations. Such dignity." Or take the time June had to say, "Golly, Bullwinkle, gee!," and it came out, "Golly, Ball-wankle…"

Conrad clears his throat. "You can say 'Bullwinkle,' can't you?" he asks in tones of tender mock concern.

THERE'S NOT MUCH TO RECOMMEND IT, BUT IT BEATS WRITING!

"I guess not," she replies in a tiny voice.

"The girl can't work sober," Conrad says gruffly, repeating one of his favorite themes. "Why don't you get a coupla belts? Will somebody belt her, please?"

Or take the time that an exasperated Conrad, having blown three straight takes of a single line, said in a tone of unappreciated high dudgeon, "You know, Adolph Menjou has a place for me in *his* organization."

"You bet he has," Ward shoots back from the control room, "behind bars."

LEAD ON, BILLY BOY!

TO THE PLOT

There's a John Cheever-ish fracture in the animation-studio fairy tale that Jim Critchfield, a writer who worked on *George of the Jungle* and *Fractured Flickers* in the mid-sixties, remembers:

"Well, we all wandered in around ten-thirty or eleven. Some of us drank quite a lot. Jay would sort of make the rounds, hoping we would all show up….Jay's vice wasn't booze, it was food. Sugar, that was our common denominator. We put in a soda fountain and popcorn makers and all of that stuff, and we would just consume a hell of a lot of ice cream and candy….He was always laughing, and to some of us he was known as the Phantom Giggler.

"You'd read him a piece of material and he'd laugh and laugh and laugh while you were reading it, but as soon as you were finished, he'd say, 'I don't think so.' "

Hollywood craftspeople might call it making history of a dubious sort, but when *Rocky* became the first animated series drawn outside of the United States, it was indisputably the beginning of a trend. Today, labor-intensive animation drawing is routinely shipped overseas.

Back then, though, setting up in Mexico City to save money was brand-new, something "the client," i.e., the sponsor, insisted on, and the man who set up the ad hoc Mexico City animation studio was veteran animation director Bill Hurtz. Even then, he went "way back," Hurtz recollects, with Bill Scott, who, as a teenager trying to get into animation, had been his "in-betweener" — that is, the person who "fills in" between the main animator's drawings.

He remembers the young Scott as "sort of the court jester. He roared out cartoons. He'd come in Monday morning after some weekend escapade."

After four months in Mexico, Hurtz came back with the "first episode and a case of hepatitis," he says. "I had to stay in bed six months."

As the process evolved, Jay and Bill, the other writers, and L.A.–based directors wrote the story lines and dialogue, then did "storyboards, tracks, and direction," Hurtz explains; in Mexico City the animators "interpreted what we sent down and they would animate it, paint it, do the background, shoot it, and send it back and we would put in the effects."

Although Ward reconciled himself to the process for economic reasons, says Hurtz, he never really cared for the results.

"Sometimes the characters would be walking along, and there'd be

WELL, CRITCH..
WHERE DO WE PUT
THE PASTRY MACHINE?

a panoramic background, and it would turn out they were walking across the top of a roof. Sometimes (the Mexico City animators') naiveté in their work was an asset: We had a forest fire [scene] once and they did it between two drawings, and we were just popping back and forward between the two. It made for a very violent and exciting forest fire. So, by accident, some of the stuff worked very well."

THE GREAT STATEHOOD-
FOR-MOOSYLVANIA SCAM

THE BULLWINKLE PICNIC
AT THE PLAZA

AND OTHER OUTRAGEOUS PROMOTIONS

It wasn't just a second banana on a popular TV variety show of the period who took Rocky and Bullwinkle's more topical gags amiss. None other than Red Skelton, then a beloved national figure with an immensely popular weekly TV show, took umbrage at Bullwinkle's gallumping voice, which sounded suspiciously like one of the comedian's own gallery of country bumpkins.

Network censors, too, steamed when Rocky and Bullwinkle found themselves in a cartoon cannibal's pot. So the Wardsters worked the reprobation into the script, having Rocky stop the stew with a well-timed network memo on cannibalism's inappropriateness over the airwaves. And on a later episode, with our heroes tied to a stake, narrator Conrad intoned, *"And as the network-approved flames leaped higher and higher!"*

Very early in the show's initial run, on ABC, during the brief period when the various cartoon adventures were being introduced by a Bullwinkle puppet (and long before remote controls came into use), the Moose once suggested to the kids watching at home that pulling the knobs off the set was a good way *"we'll be sure to be with you next week."*

When children all across the country did exactly that, the network brass were furious, and Bullwinkle had to come back with a retraction. But the Moose's delivery wasn't exactly contrite: *"Remember, kids, a coupla weeks ago we asked you to pull the knobs off your sets? Well, you can put them back on now. Use glue — and make it stick."*

In one episode Natasha stops Boris from shooting our heroes by reminding the Pottsylvanian baddie that TV violence — an issue then as it is now — is no longer allowed. When he replies, *"But I could swear — "* she cuts him off with *"Not on this program, dollink."*

Another time, when Natasha, who has her trusty switchblade nail file at the ready, drolly observes to Boris, who's just been crushed by a falling treasure chest, *"Don't worry, dollink, it's just a cartoon,"* Boris replies: *"I just found out vot happens vhen a cartoon chest falls on a cartoon character....It hurts!"*

And in yet another episode, when Rocky wonders why they're being shot at, Bullwinkle naturally supposes that it's a rival network. Similar examples abound. In fact, one of the elements that distinguished *Rocky and Bullwinkle* from most other TV cartoon fare, both then and now, is that the characters were excruciatingly aware of themselves as not only cartoon characters, but as TV stars and show-business performers as well, arguing with the narrator, and slipping knowing asides into outlandish stories in much the same way that in movies Groucho Marx and the Hope and Crosby of the Road pictures would at times break the "fourth wall" to talk directly to the audience.

Says Rocket J.: *"Do you know what an A-bomb is?"*

Replies Mister Moose: *"Certainly. A bomb is what some people call our program."*

"I don't think that's so funny," Rocky replies with that customary touch of boyish petulance.

Shoots back the moose: *"Neither do they, apparently!"*

Immediately the narrator intones: *"And while our two heroes engage in airy persiflage, the villains are on their way!..."*

And on yet another occasion Rocky professes to be worried, which causes the moose to wonder if the ratings are down again. But the heroic flying squirrel, concerned about his big pal's safety, persists:

"There've already been two attempts on your life!"

"Don't worry," assures the sanguine Bullwinkle, *"we'll be renewed."*

And somewhat later in the same adventure, when the narrator worries if there's no way to stop the bad guys, Boris says smugly, *"Only eef the show is canceled, buddy."*

The narrator, himself savvy about the ways of Hollywood, shrugs verbally and tells Boris, in that case, to go ahead with his dastardly scheme.

And on yet a later occasion, when Rocky, Bullwinkle, and Boris do their that-voice-where-have-I-heard-it-before routine, Bullwinkle allows that they've heard it "in about three hundred and twenty-four other episodes...but I don't know who it is either."

All the while, particularly after the show made its transition from ABC to NBC, the frequent mailers to some two thousand "opinion makers" on the Wardsters' mailing list, the pop-culture gags (such as having actresses dressed as Salvation Army ladies march down Madison Avenue with signs aloft proclaiming REPENT! WATCH THE BULLWINKLE SHOW), and the other promotions continued, bringing an enormous amount of press attention to the show. Why?

The promotions were "incredibly funny," says gravel-voiced Howard Brandy, Jay Ward's longtime press agent, and – says he – the prognathous-jawed model for Dudley Do-Right.

As for Ward – who in late 1963 made Brandy don a Dudley Do-Right Royal Canadian Mountie costume, complete with hat, and drive him all around the country in a Ford truck transformed into a circus wagon, complete with calliope, collecting more than thirty thousand Statehood for Moosylvania petition signatures (and much local newspaper ink for *The Bullwinkle Show*) – the press agent fondly says: "He was just a big kid."

From 1961 onward, once the show had made the move to the Peacock Network, the Kid told his wife "he was going to do a lot of promotions. He spent a lot of time on that," Ramona Ward recalls. "He had lists and lists of people I'd never heard about – [people] in the business....He got a kick out of the mailers and he *loved* planning all of the different promotions."

One memorably fractured 1963 do, for example, ended up costing Ward himself upward of fifty thousand dollars, she says.

To properly send off *Fractured Flickers,* an ahead-of-its-time camped-up marriage of old silent movies and dubbed-in wisecracking dialogue, Ward decided he needed to hire Coney Island for the evening. He then rented two ten-car subway trains that "actually started out from [the] Forty-second Street [station], if you can believe it," says Ramona Ward, who herself was dolled up as a twenties flapper for the occasion.

At the station, she says, were "old-fashioned bath-tubs with legs," each filled with the trademark Ward giveaways – this time, hats, perfume, feather boas, headbands, necklaces, long Natasha-like slinky ciga-rette holders, et cetera. None other than legendary drummer Gene Krupa was there to greet the bedazzled crowd of usual suspects – show folk mixed with ink-stained wretches – as they descended into the Times Square underground; and on the Coney Island end of the subway ride the greeters were real Brooklyn Dodgers in their baseball uniforms.

Naturally, each car was stocked with food and drink, and a "half-block-long speakeasy bar" awaited the

FLASH!

A BULLETIN FROM BULLWINKLE NEWS

10 NOVEMBER, 1961

Regular viewers of "The Bullwinkle Show" are familiar with a remarkable piece of headgear known as the "Kirward Derby", which gives its wearer enormous intellectual properties. A well-known TV announcer and personality, whose name bears a startling resemblance to that of the famous hat, has seen the humor of the situation and, in an effort to join in the fun ... is suing us!

While his and our attorneys are out haggling, we'd like to invite Mr. Kirby to feel free to name one of his hats after any one of the characters on "The Bullwinkle Show", including the producers, Jay Ward and Bill Scott. Toward this end, we are sending Mr. Kirby a Bullwinkle Beanie. We hope he will wear it in good health.

guests when they arrived at Coney Island, Ramona Ward says, still bubbling at the memory: "The best hot dogs, I still love them today, the foot-long ones [and] real bathtub gin served out of bathtubs....

"Then it started to rain." She remembers a deluge of biblical proportions, with water puddling ankle-high, the Ferris wheel brought to a lazy stop and a private plane crashing in flames nearby. But none of it dimmed the festivities.

"There were a lot of big tents...and several jazz bands...so we pushed the tables together and we danced on [them], and a band was up on the chairs."

The party didn't break up until the next morning. "To this day, people still come in [to the Dudley Do-Right Emporium] and say, 'I was there.'"

How far did they take the Statehood-for-Moosylvania campaign? Admiral Ward actually dispatched his trusted aide, longtime editor Skip Craig, to Minnesota with a signed blank check and a mandate: *Find an island, buy it, call it Moosylvania!*

"The wildest thing that ever happened to me," the behind-the-scenes show business veteran recalls, "is that Moosylvania thing. Because I came from a small town in Minnesota, he sent me back there to buy an island. He was going to proclaim it Moosylvania and apply for statehood....So I go back, get my uncle [he used to be a surveyor] and we go up...start going through the map books. Almost all the islands are on the Canadian side; he wanted something American. There were hundreds on the Canadian side, only seven or fourteen or something like that on the American. So we started tracking down the owners. Some of them thought we were crazy and wouldn't talk to us. Finally we found this dentist, he was a pretty hip guy and thought the whole thing was hilarious."

The final cost of the Moosylvania Purchase?

Fifteen hundred dollars for a three-year lease. Cost paid, of course — as were the out-of-pocket expenses for countless other, sometimes lavish, promotions — by none other than Admiral Ward himself. As his wife so succinctly put it, "Jay always [said] you should spare no expense for a good joke."

Moosylvania figured, as well, in two Rocky and Bullwinkle adventures, "Statehood for Moosylvania" and "Moosylvania Saved."

What kind of a place is it? According to an entry in *Poor Jay's Almanac,* declaimed by our Narrator in his trademark, rapid-fire, and breathlessly clipped voice-of-doom staccato, it's a "small land adjacent to the United States...zero people, zero production, zero space development, zero everything; but on the other hand, no taxes, no laws, no traffic, no extradition treaties and no late

traffic, no extradition treaties and no late shows." Its governor: none other than Bullwinkle J. Moose himself, currently – and prudently – a resident of nearby Frostbite Falls, Minnesota.

While Jay and Howard were rattling around the country, Rocky and Bullwinkle's cartoon campaign took them directly to Butte, Montana. Well, not actually. Perhaps Boris Badenov's most fiendish plan of all was to disguise Butte as Washington, D.C., complete with a green Frankenstein statue atop the U.S. Capitol. But, it transpires that our heroes are in the real Washington after all, the place they'd set out for, because it turns out that Washington had been first disguised as Butte by the Montana Musk Melon Trust, which was trying to curry favor with Congress. Got it? But the venal politicos are not to be so easily swayed.

"Son," drawls a bourbon-and-branchwater-voiced senator to a disappointed Musk Melon lobbyist, "ah even voted against Medicare, and *they* wrapped fifty-four million Band-Aids around the Washington Monument."

Meanwhile, on a very particular early fall-season day, Jay Ward's Statehood-for-Moosylvania campaign also reached the city on the Potomac, taking him and Howard, resplendent in their respective Napoleonic admiral and Canadian Mountie costumes, to the very gate of the White House.

But before recounting the next episode in their adventure, and revealing the dread shock that awaited them at journey's end, let's sneak a peek at a few more pages from the last word on matters Moosylvanian, *Poor Jay's Almanac,* unseen since the height of the cold war, when postage stamps cost a mere four copper pennies (so *that's* what

they used to use those little brown coins for!) and moosle bases – that is, *missile* bases – were on everyone's mind.

THE MOOSYLVANIA STORY

The United States today is plagued by problems of international politics, brushfire wars, internal dissension, and world economic discord. To these gnawing problems was added this week the flea bite of a plea for admission to statehood by the unincorporated territory of Moosylvania, an indeterminate area lying somewhere between Minnesota and Canada. Moosylvania's boundaries have not yet been clearly determined due to the tendency of the marshy ground to swallow up surveying instruments – and surveyors.

However, in the words of its chief spokesman, Governor Bullwinkle Moose, "The federal guvmmint has dillydallied too long. We must take action! Our plans for progress have long been delayed! It's time they were expedited! And like that."

Part of the reason for Moosylvania's lack of recognition as a state lies in the fact that at present nobody lives there. "Makes no nevermind," says Governor Moose, who makes *his* home in Frostbite Falls, Minnesota. "A state shouldn't be looked down on just because it's got a population problem. Actually, Moosylvanians show a higher intelligence than residents of many other states. When *they* don't like a place, they move out!" As a result, Moosylvania has the largest absentee population of any place on earth. Moose is also quick to point out that many of those who extoll the beauties of southern states live in New York and Chicago. "You can allus be a better citizen when you're some-wheres else," he says.

There are many reasons advanced as to why nobody lives in Moosylvania. First, its winter climate is rather brisk, though in some warmer years the temperature has risen to as high as twenty degrees – below zero. As a result, the Moosylvanian spring thaw sets in about the 25th of September, and the first snow falls in the middle of October. The brief summer, though, is filled with the hum-ming of thousands of wings – the wings of Moosylvania's mammoth mosquitoes, two of which have been taken to Texas to be used in experimental oil-well drilling.

A second reason for the lack of large cities is that a large proportion of Moosylvania is frozen over most of the year and underwater the rest. "No worse'n Florida," snaps Bullwinkle, "and we don't have sand chiggers, neither."

Moosylvania is at present asking for U.S. aid in the amount of eighteen billion dollars and four cents (They insist the government pay for the postage for its own check) to be spent for industrial development and civic improvement within the state, including a multimillion-dollar freeway system. "If we plan it right," says Bullwinkle, "people who don't like Moosylvania will be able to drive clear through it without stopping once. No other state in the nation is that considerate!"

Much has been made of the fact that Moosylvania wants to be the fifty-*second* state to join the Union. When

asked if his state was deferring to Puerto Rico, Bullwinkle declared, "Heck no! We figure Puerto Rico is a state already. But we'd like *Texas* to join up before we do." But there are other reasons why Moosylvania supporters want fifty-two states in the Union. "It's just neater some-how. Just think, you could put out pictures-of-the-states playing cards without offending anybody," says Bullwinkle, who just happens to own the Ajax Playing Card Company. "Our motto is 'A full deck for the U.S.A.!'"

The future of life in Moosylvania looks intriguing, to say the least. "We want Moosylvania to be just a little bit dif-ferent," says Bullwinkle. "In Moosylvania, for instance, the *government* will go to work every day and pay taxes to the *people*." But some of Moosylvania's most interesting proposals lie in the field of entertainment. Its proposed phonograph record industry, for example, will feature only singers who have passed their sixty-fifth birth-day. "It's time we stopped catering to teenagers and did something for the social security set,"

November 8th, 1962

President of the United States,
The Honorable John F. Kennedy,
White House,
Washington, D.C.

Dear Mr. President:

In my official capacity as National Chairman of the "Statehood for Moosylvania" Committee, and on behlf of the citizens of Moosylvania, I hereby petition the President and the Congress of the United States of America to admit the unincorporated territory of Moosylvania into the Union as the 52nd State.

I am enclosing the proposed Constitution of Moosylvania and copies of the petitions signed by many of our non-resident population. More and more petitions are coming into our office every day and I venture to say that we will have a half million citizens of Moosylvania by the end of the year.

Thanks for your consideration in this matter. I'm also enclosing a decal for use on your Presidential car.

Very truly yours,

Jay Ward,
Chairman, "Statehood for Moosylvania"
Committee,
8218 Sunset Boulevard,
Hollywood, California

avers Governor Moose. "Besides, some of them old folks are *loaded!*"

Also, in an avowed effort to "give the people what they want," Moosylvanian television will present a daily program appealing to the public's love of audience participation shows, games of chance, and violence. On the program, called *Loser Take All,* a housewife will be chosen by lottery from the studio audience and slowly beaten to death onstage. Moose figures that if the program can be done in color with a score by Hank Mancini, it will get a sensational Nielsen, besides thinning the ranks of housewives in studio audiences. "And you know how they been mountin' up," says the governor.

One of the chief advantages of locating in Moosylvania is that it is one of the few spots anywhere that is absolutely unsuitable for a missile base – or anything else for that matter. "If the balloon goes up," says Governor Moose, "we figure to be the only place in the world nobody's aiming at!"

The government of Moosylvania will be set up using a strict two-party system. One party will start at nine and the other at eleven-thirty. Both will break up at five A.M. some future morning. Under state law, campaigning politicians will not be allowed to kiss any babies under eighteen years of age. They will, however, have access to a complete set of applause, cheering, and laugh tracks for use during political rallies. This will do away with the need for getting lots of people together in one place, a necessary measure since whenever two people stand on one piece of Moosylvania real estate, the heavier of them begins to sink.

The mushy landscape, however, is deemed no deterrent to the building of the proposed hundred-million-dollar airport. Indeed, even the present landing field boasts a ten-thousand-foot runway. Unfortunately, only eighteen percent of it is on solid land – but arriving passengers are disembarked from their aircraft in gaily painted municipal yachts, recently purchased from the Central Park rowboat concession. When asked if planes might not have trouble taking off again, Governor Moose replied, "Possible, yes. But we're banking on the idea that once people get here, they won't want to leave."

If people *do* want to leave, though, Moosylvania is ready. In addition to the proposed freeways, there is a proposed railway network and a proposed statewide subway system. At present, however, all transportation is by birchbark canoe. "But we're in step with the times," adds the governor proudly. "We're usin' double-bladed paddles!" Other forms of communication among Moosylvanians are nearly as advanced. Already an enterprising Minnesota telephone company has installed a party line that reaches a candy store quite close to the border. Just leave a message.

As a spur to colonization of this frontier empire, Governor Moose has outlined the Moosylvanian program of tax relief. This program consists of only one item: there will be no extradition treaty with the federal government. "We want Moosylvania to be a place where a man can spend his golden years," says Bullwinkle. "Also all that loot." To protect its integrity against possible interference by other less broadminded states, the Moosylvanian State Guard is being organized and equipped with the latest-model slingshots.

The state's motto, based upon its many treacherous quicksand bogs, is "Don't Tread on Me."

The first issue of the state's only newspaper, *The Moose Call,* has just come off the presses. A good five years ahead of its time, the *Call* includes a full twenty-eight pages of comic strips, lovelorn columns, and horoscopes, and one page of world news sandwiched just ahead of the want ad section.

But perhaps the most daring part of Moosylvania's program for the future lies in its method of appointing ambassadors – for no Moosylvanian ambassador may be a resident of the state. The reason behind this extraordinary practice is a simple one, according to an off-the-record statement by Governor Moose. "It's just that nobody who's ever seen the place has a good word for it!" As a result, ambassadors are being appointed from the ranks of Broadway and Hollywood columnists, ad agency and network executives, and any others whose daily work keeps them far away from Moosylvania.

The ambassadorship includes an engraved scroll, the medal of the Honorary Order of Moosylvania Mudders (which alone is worth its weight in cardboard), and a red sash for wearing with formal dress (it can also be used to tie Christmas packages). Millions of eager applicants have already requested ambassadorships from this progressive pesthole, though only one has been appointed so far. He is Milton Fugg of Upper Darby, PA. The choice of Fugg as number-one ambassador was based on many things – his obvious intelligence and eagerness, his spotless background – and also he was the only applicant to enclose a self-addressed stamped envelope.

Moosylvania supporters have already grown testy at the lack of a reply to their demands. "If the United States won't heed our just pleas," says the governor darkly, "we may be forced to look elsewhere for aid." Seasoned observers are at a loss to know who else might be interested in the state. Canada has twice refused the area as an outright gift, even with Lake Superior thrown in; and the Communist bloc has denied any interest in the territory. "We're out to grab whatever we can," says a noted Red spokesman, "but there are *some* things you just don't squeeze with your bare hands."

※ ◎ ✺ ℓ ℓ ◎ ✴

"We were just two guys in strange costumes," says publicist Brandy of the Moosylvania cross-country road trip. "I mean, we were constantly stopped by police on Main Street in all these small towns [we traveled through]."

They drove from small town to small town – Brandy as Do-Right and Ward in his comic-opera admiral's get-up – playing calliope music from the picturesquely decorated truck in impromptu parades that snarled traffic on many a main street, all the while gathering signatures and dropping in at the NBC affiliate station in each city and hamlet on their meandering way, until, more than thirty thousand signatures later and after several weeks on the road, one bright day they reached Washington, D.C.

In full regalia and with circus music blaring, they drove right up to the White House gate. Brandy remembers the historic moment this way:

"The guard says, 'Whaddya guys want?' and Jay says, 'We wanna see President Kennedy, we have this petition for statehood for Moosylvania.'

"The guard says, *'Get out!'* and Jay says, 'You don't have to be mean, we're just asking.' And the guard says, 'You got till the counta three to get outta here,' and he begins unflapping his gun belt.

"I'm screaming, 'Jay, let's get outta here!' and Jay says, 'Well, he could at least be decent, he didn't have to be so rude about it,' and he starts to lecture this [White House] cop, and I'm saying, 'Jay, *please,* let's get outta here.'

"So he backs [the truck] out, muttering, and I'm going, 'Jay, *puh-leeze,* do you see that guy? He's crazed! He's ready to take that gun out of his holster!'

"And Jay says [huffily], 'Well, he could've done anything he liked, but he was a rude guy, and *I* don't like rudeness.'

"Jay always took this moral stand, and he was genuinely hurt by [the guard's attitude]."

So like the good press agent that he was, Brandy dropped into the Washington office of the Associated Press. After he related the story of the rude and hostile White House reception, an editor there showed him some just-in photos: high-altitude spy plane photos of…

Russian Missiles in Cuba

"We're going to be at war in twenty-four hours," the AP man averred.

Oops, thought Brandy. They had arrived at the White House on the first day of the Cuban Missile Crisis. You could call it the ultimate fiendish plan.

But the Master Promoters weren't done yet. With the crisis averted and the world safely intact, they did what came naturally, according to Ramona Ward, calling several press conferences around the country to issue mea culpas – was the Moosylvanian campaign in bad taste, given that World War III had just been narrowly averted? Inquiring minds wanted to know.

Of course, Jay agreed genially, and Ramona Ward fervently concurs: "He would never have done it [shown up at the White House on that fateful day] if he'd known. But he didn't know it, and it turned out to be quite a publicity thing," she declares, remembering that he told her then "how embarrassing it was and they were actually *very scared.* I mean, here were people with sidearms, rifles, guns *pointing at them* and surrounding the car. It was a frightening experience."

But it wasn't long before they were back at it: The flurry of post-near-apocalypse press conferences were followed after a few days by a midtown Manhattan pre-Thanksgiving Moose's Day Parade that snarled traffic while the hundreds of invited show business and media figures wended their way to Sardi's, a swank restaurant. There they dined not on the regular bill of fare, but in typically irreverent Jay Ward fashion, on burgers and hot dogs served up by pushcart vendors.

The guests, expecting something slightly more upscale at the fancy restaurant, were nonetheless mollified by a free-flowing no-host bar (with Jay picking up the tab) and such giveaways as derby hats accessorized with antlers.

"I was in that parade," says Ramona Ward. "They had carloads of convertible cars filled with Playboy bunnies, a flatbed truck with a marching band on it... a lot of Broadway show people. I must've served several cases of champagne."

Apparently, the Great Moosylvania Mishap had resulted in a new maturity when it came to those pesky parade permits. "He got permits for this one," Ramona Ward confirms. "It cost him a lot of money, it cost him a lot of watches."

Watches? "Oh, yes, Bullwinkle watches, the real good hand-painted ones, and I think probably cases of champagne. Things flowed *very rapidly* for the permits."

Appropriately enough for the man who'd campaigned to make Moosylvania the fifty-*second* state [Mississippi, he always said, in a not-so-veiled reference to the civil rights struggles of the time, would eventually become the fifty-first], Jay Ward threw his New Year's '63 party in New York on March 19 – a mere three months late.

The festivities were held at the Improv, and all the Moose Day Parade participants were invited. "They celebrated New Year's [several] times that night," says Ramona Ward, who missed this one herself. "I guess to have more fun, more drinks, more toasts. They had [the New Year's revelry] at eleven o'clock, they had it at 12:47 [A.M.], and they had it at 1:15 and 3:30 [in the morning]." The traditional bill of fare included six-foot-long hero sandwiches and spaghetti.

Not a month later, Ward was back to take another bite out of the Big Apple with a Homecoming Party at Columbia University – naturally *not* his alma mater.

But he wasn't one to be dissuaded by a detail like that. Instead, says Ramona Ward, "he donated a good bit of money to the university."

And before you could say twenty three-skiddoo there were the usual matriculators – this time raccoon-coated

Senator at Large
The holder of this card has been duly appointed as a representative of the creatures of the Unincorporated Territory of
MOOSYLVANIA

or in striped jackets and straw boaters, surrounded by scantily dressed coeds, and one memorably dressed young lady done up in leopard skins who was to be found in a six-foot-tall animal cage. "You could feed [her]," says the very proper Mrs. Ward, "but you couldn't get too close."

The great Statehood-for-Moosylvania scam wasn't the only time a Rocky and Bullwinkle promotion took a cartoon whack upside the real world. The nonstop mailings to columnists and other "opinion-makers," the high-profile gags and the extravagant events were all *about* the real world; they tweaked and twisted it, though, especially the already bizarre and basically *un*real, though related, realms of politics and show business. And the Wardsters got back *loads* of attention, not all of it pleased, from show biz insiders and politicos alike.

Consider, for example, the Newton Minow mailer. Mr. Minow, of course, was the Federal Communications Commissioner who coined the term "vast wasteland" to describe early-sixties TV. When Minow called for less TV violence, Ward and company replied with a TV show "gift pak" offer, which included, for the bargain price of six hundred and thirty thousand dollars, show pak #557C, the "Newton Minow pak," consisting of *Peter Watergun* ("a private eye with a new gimmick"), *Championship Hopscotch* ("an ideal replacement for the Saturday night fights"), and *Hamlet* ("the Danish prince and his uncle the king are able to resolve their differences and Ophelia does nicely after a few visits to her

psychiatrist"). To those who ordered two or more Minow paks, Ward promised to throw in a free pamphlet, "1001 Ways to Lose Your FCC License."

The real Minow really replied: "I am intrigued by your #557C. Please consider this an order for three paks. I understand that with two or more orders, you will send me absolutely free your pamphlet."

History does not record if Minow actually received said pamphlet or if he ever actually paid for his three-pak bargain order. History does record, however, the running battle between Jay Ward and a network, NBC, that when it came to Rocky and Bullwinkle and "getting it," was ambivalent at best. In fact, according to a number of Ward's one-time colleagues, the network rarely picked up the sometimes-considerable tab for the mailers and the other promotions — not surprising, perhaps, given how often those tongue-in-cheek press releases took dead aim at the peacock.

In view of the fact that Bullwinkle's crusade for statehood for Moosylvania has thus far been somewhat less than a superbly magnificent success in the halls of the United States Congress and among certain selfish interest groups, all Moosylvanians must galvanize their efforts and steel themselves for further action in the year – 1963. To do this we invite you to stop by your local embassy for training and conditioning in the great and noble game of Farkling – a terse but illuminating insight into this national sport may be gleaned from the following:

"The farkler's bludgeon may not exceed 36" in length and 25 lbs. in weight, as it is feared that a blow delivered by an instrument in excess of these dimensions might be a trifle dangerous. If the referee calls a foul or "Bingo," the offensive quarter-tackle is allowed two free swings below the belt of the opposing captain or a single pistol shot into the cheering section. The match ends when five of the six teams involved are completely wiped out or one team has Monopoly."

(Rules, Scoring, and Penalties same as Zudirk)

State Flower: Moosylvanian flytrap "A botanical curiosity, they are the only plants known to belch."

```
WHAT CAN THE PUBLIC DO TO HELP????? WELL FOR ONE THING, THEY
CAN SHOUT OUT "STATEHOOD FOR MOOSYLVANIA" AT THE CRUCIAL POINT
IN MOTION PICTURES IN THEIR LOCAL THEATERS!

PARTICIPANTS MUST, HOWEVER, ONLY SHOUT AT SPECIFIED PLACES IN
CURRENT FILMS. FAILURE TO SHOUT WHERE WE TELL YOU TO SHOUT WILL
RESULT IN A BREAKDOWN OF OUR WHOLE SCHEME AND THE LOSS OF OUR
RESPECT FOR YOU NO MATTER HOW MUCH YOU LIKE US.

"STATEHOOD FOR MOOSYLVANIA" CAN BE SHOUTED ONLY IN THE FOLLOWING
PLACES IN THE FOLLOWING PICTURES:

      THE MIRACLE WORKER.
           Just as Hellen finally and ardigiously says her
      first words by the water pump (near end of picture.
      Now remember, we're counting on you to wait).

      WEST SIDE STORY
           Just as Chino shoots Tony in final sceen on the
      tennis court. Try to lip-sinc to Chino's warning.

      MUTINY ON THE BOUNTY
           As Brando fixes a breadfruitberger.

      ATTILLA THE HUN
           Feel free to yell whenever you think Attilla looks
      swishy.

      HERCULES UNCHAINED
           When Steve Reeves removes his teeth and gums a
      lyon to death.

      BUTTERFIELD 8
           Just as Liz tells her mom she was really Tokyo Rose
      during the war.
```

We have a favor to ask...

Jay Ward Productions, the people responsible for the new "Bullwinkle Show" (starts September 24, 7:00 PM, EST, NBC, Color) would like to enlist your help in the promotion of their exciting new show.

During the week prior to the premiere performance of "The Bullwinkle Show", we would like you to go naked.

When you see others in their offices, on the street, in restaurants, etc., without their clothes, you will instantly know that they too are helping to promote the Bullwinkle Show!

Why?

    1. It will attract a great deal of attention.

    2. By the end of the week, everyone will be aware of the new "Bullwinkle Show".

    3. It's fun.

    4. It's a conversation piece.

So don't forget. Get those clothes off during the entire week preceeding the big opening show ———— Sunday night, September 24!

The Bullwinkle Show   NBC

the bullwinkle show • nbc

Please watch the premiere of "THE BULLWINKLE SHOW", then complete the form below and return to us. Failure to complete this form will give you an automatic "F" for the semester.

CHECK ONE:

1. *What feature of "The Bullwinkle Show" did you enjoy most?*

    a.) *Commercials* _____
    b.) *Dudley Do-Right* _____
    c.) *Closing credits* _____
    d.) *Elsa Maxwell strip-tease* _____
    e.) *Crocodile-pirahna fight* _____
    f.) *Other* _____

2. *Concerning the use of profanity, do you think there was:*

    a.) *too much* _____
    b.) *not enough* _____
    c.) *just enough* _____

3. *Who is your favorite character on "The Bullwinkle Show"*

    a.) *Bullwinkle* _____
    b.) *Boris* _____
    c.) *Jimmy Hoffa* _____
    d.) *Rocky* _____
    e.) *Leonard Bernstein* _____
    f.) *Other* _____

4. *Which word do you think best describes the show?*

    a.) *funny* _____
    b.) *overrated* _____
    c.) *half-hour* _____
    d.) *trivial* _____
    e.) *fetid* _____
    f.) *antidisestablishmentarianistic* _____

5. *Where did you watch "The Bullwinkle Show"?*

    a.) *home* _____
    b.) *office* _____
    c.) *bar* _____
    d.) *TV store window* _____
    e.) *warden's office* _____
    f.) *none of your business* _____

6. *Would you watch it again:*

    a.) *regularly* _____
    b.) *over your dead body?* _____
    c.) *if it were the last show on TV?* _____
    d.) *if your life depended on it?* _____

7. *What would you like to see more of on "The Bullwinkle Show"?*

    a.) *roller skating* _____
    b.) *Winston Churchill* _____
    c.) *chamber music* _____
    d.) *commercials* _____

Give yourself 2 points for every answer. If you scored from 12—14 points you have our permission to watch next week's show.

Thinking of killing yourself?

STOP!   WAIT!   THINK IT OVER!

Why do it for nothing when you can earn BIG MONEY or FABULOUS PRIZES for helping to promote "The Bullwinkle Show"?

Here's how it works. Our promotion department has thought up some marvelous stunts to publicize "The Bullwinkle Show", but they can only be carried out by YOU, the potential suicide. CONTACT US IMMEDIATELY! GO OUT WITH A FLOURISH!

Here a just a few of the exciting ways to choose from:

1. *Crash a 1938 Hudson Terraplane ("The Bullwinkle Special") into Lenin's Tomb in Red Square!*

2. *Hit Mao Tse-tung in the face with a bowl of tomato chow yuk while yelling "Bullwinkle!" and the time and day of the show!*

3. *Go over Niagara Falls in a moose suit!*

4. *Soak Fidel Castro's beard with gasoline, using your Bullwinkle Official Water Pistol! Also yell "Bullwinkle si, tractors no!"*

5. *Scream "Thank you, General Sarnoff, sir!" while hurling past his window after leaping from the top of the RCA Building. The show's producers are grateful for their excellent time slot and would like to show it.*

6. *Be buried alive in the forecourt of Grauman's Chinese Theatre at the press preview of "The Bullwinkle Show"!*

And many, many more. Don't do anything until you've talked to us. CALL NOW! Operators on duty 24 hours a day. And call COLLECT!

JayWard Prods.

The heroically posed Rocky and Bullwinkle statue across from the Chateau Marmont on the Sunset Strip may or may not be one of the Great Wonders of the World. That's a question best left for semiologists and other philosophers.

But the statue's unveiling, timed to coincide with the fall season 1961 premiere of *The Bullwinkle Show* on NBC was indisputably one humdinger of a party.

Originally, the statue was Dudley Do-Right's idea — or so says publicist Howard Brandy, the kind of guy *Variety* might describe as a "praiser extraordinaire."

"I went to see Jay and I said, 'I've always wanted a statue, so let's build a statue of Bullwinkle,' and he said, 'That's a wonderful idea,'" Brandy recalls. "Jay says, 'I always wanted to do a takeoff of Grauman's [now Mann's] Chinese Theatre. Instead of handprints let's do drinking elbows.' So we had the various cognizant people who Jay loved put their [bent] drinking elbows in concrete [around the base of the Rocky and Bullwinkle statue]."

Those bent-elbow prints are there to this day, and so is the statue, after more than three decades still a Hollywood fixture, next door to the Dudley Do-Right Emporium, marking the eastern border of the Sunset Strip.

Originally, though, the statue rotated on its base, turning in ironic sync with another statue right across the boulevard — a spangly, sexy showgirl in a bikini and cowboy hat who was advertising the Sahara Hotel and Casino in Las Vegas. For the Rocky and Bullwinkle statue's grand unveiling, Ward and company managed the rather unlikely feat of having all but a single lane of busy Sunset Boulevard closed to automobile traffic (in typical Ward fashion, a sign advised motorists to stop complaining "Or We'll Block *This* Lane Too!") and threw a block party attended by thousands.

Bill Hurtz, who'd earlier set up the Mexican animation studio, still chuckles at the memory: "The evening they dedicated the statue in front of the studio, Jay and Bill [Scott] were in top hats, tails, and tennis shoes, and [fifties sexpot] Jayne Mansfield pulled the ribbon dropping the canvas [covering the statue]."

And to this day, a trace of the wide-eyed awe he felt as a boy at that block party creeps into the now grown-up voice of Jay Ward's youngest son, Carey. "*Jayne Mansfield*...she was the *only* thing I wanted to see!"

But a few weeks before the extravagant block party there was a Bullwinkle fall season premiere, done in typical Hollywood fashion — with searchlights cutting through the night sky, celebrities promenading down a plush red carpet, the whole soigné works, with a madcap Ward twist. Invited celebrities were ignored, while the unsung wretches of the Fourth Estate were greeted with delirious cheers from a hidden, behind-the-scenes audio system. Ward and Scott, naturally, came dressed to kill, attired in white tie, tails, shorts, and tennis shoes.

"Yes, he was walking down Sunset Boulevard in his underwear, tails, and a top hat and sneakers," says Ramona Ward, a tall, attractive, and rather dignified woman whom everyone calls Billie. She shakes her head in mock disapproval at the impropriety of it all. "People would turn around. I was embarrassed. Yes."

But she was Jay Ward's wife. That practically guaranteed there would be further embarrassments ahead.

PLAN ZANY PARTY FOR BULLWINKLE

Hollywood's famed Sunset Strip, scene of gala nightclub activity, is in for a switch Wednesday night — a good old-fashioned "block party."

Producers Jay Ward and Bill Scott are throwing the shindig to honor Bullwinkle J. Moose, star of their color cartoon series, "The Bullwinkle Show," which starts on NBC-TV Sunday, Sept. 24.

The party will celebrate the unveiling of one of the most unusual statues ever erected in Hollywood — a likeness of Bullwinkle 30 feet tall. Mounted on a revolving pedestal, it will be lighted by four spotlights at one of the strategic locations on the strip, Bullwinkle's "home" (the Ward office at 8218 Sunset Boulevard).

The block party will center in front of Ward's offices, and stretch along the Strip to nearby Havenhurst Drive, which will be roped off for dancing. Los Angeles county sheriff Peter J. Pitchess will unveil the statue, assisted by Jayne Mansfield.

"The Plush Pup," a popular Strip spot, has been booked for the evening, renamed "The Plush Moose," and will feature a menu of mooseburgers and malted moose milks. Sidewalk tables will lend a continental flavor to the evening.

Valley Times Today

September 18, 1961

Take the ants at the Plaza for example. The Grand Ballroom of this perennially elegant Manhattan hotel was the site of the Bullwinkle Picnic, a typically cracked, Jay Ward–financed celebration of *The Bullwinkle Show*'s first anniversary — "one of the most novel functions" ever at the Plaza, according to *The Plaza Cookbook* (Prentice-Hall, 1972), a tome otherwise dedicated to loving reminiscences of all the elaborate epicurean excellences wrought by the venerable hotel's world-class chefs for the ultra-dignified, sometimes historic affairs held there.

"The entire meal, except for the dessert," the cookbook fairly sniffs of the Bullwinkle Picnic, "was served à la box luncheon, in cartons wheeled into the ballroom on stainless steel wagons. Each guest received a box, the top of which was imprinted with the contents."

Those picnic yummies included smoked loin of pork, roast duck, and deviled disjointed chicken, as well as cold cuts, fruit, and cheese.

Dessert, served by the discreetly efficient Plaza waiters, was "vanilla ice cream in the shape of Bullwinkle's horns, topped with Brandied Strawberries Jubilee," recounts the cookbook. "In tune with the al fresco nature of the party, a Good Humor man made the rounds...."

"At cocktail hour preceding dinner, the hors d'oeuvres were Moose-Burgers Flambé, Hot Moose Dogs, and Bull Shrimp. Libations were poured from two large kegs of beer, and martinis were served from barrels set up in the foyer."

Understandably, the distinguished cookbook chooses to overlook the hired pickpocket...and those pesky ants.

"They did have caged ants," Ramona Ward confirms, deadpan. "After all, a picnic *has* to have ants, and they had red carpets, and oh, they had [hired] a pickpocket who'd walk around, pick your pocket, and then give it back."

"Jay hated the ants," says his press agent, Howard Brandy. "One of the Jay touches at the Plaza that I've always loved was, as everyone came through the door, we'd have a trumpet fanfare and a drumroll, [except] when the celebrities came in, we'd ignore it."

Another time, they set off through the streets of Manhattan in an unauthorized parade, with circus music, cartoony costumed characters, and assorted minor celebrities of the period in tow, all preceded by one of Howard Brandy's New York–based colleagues, who carried a "stack of bills that would choke a dinosaur, and as we came to a cop on the beat, he would slap a tenner in his hand," Brandy says blithely (presumably because the statute of limitations on that particular piece of puffery has expired by now), "and if that wasn't enough, he'd slap another one [down] and we'd keep moving, and that's how the parade went."

Playville Club News

VOL. I , NO. 1   Hollywood, California

JAY WARD DOES IT AGAIN!

Opens Key Clubs In 86 Cities

Here it is!! America's most exclusive key club — Jay Ward's Playville Club! Did we say exclusive? You bet! This club is so exclusive that we can't tell you the address! But don't let that discourage you — just keep trying that little key until you find us. Our second exclusive feature is really wild, we think. You notice you got two keys? Well, that's because we're the first key club in America to have another key club on the premises! Come in soon — let one of our comely "Playmooses" fetch you a bottle of Moxie or Dr. Pepper while you lounge around watching Jay Ward TV pilots in the "Projection Room". Or maybe you would like to get a client bombed in our famous "Hotbox Suite". Or perhaps you just want to have a Playmoose hold your head after the Neilsen's come out. We think you'll come to regard your Playville Club keys as highly as your washroom key. Use it often.

Some of the Playmooses at the Topeka Playville Club.

FRISKY!

"Fun Night" at the Chester (Pa.) Playville Club.

Lionel Pfaff, President of Pfaff & Pfuzz Advertising, looking for the Playville Club in his town. You're warm, Lionel!

Jay T. Ward, pioneer in the field of entertainment

CLUB KEY IS PERFECT CHRISTMAS GIFT

The Chicago club is a little difficult to find!

Abe Klutz, one of the great nightclub acts appearing at the Playville Club in Yakima, Washington.

Another smash act seen nightly at the Pismo Beach club!

Who could resist this fetching Playmoose?

Playville Club News

The Melody Belles —— favorites at the Playville Club in Detroit.

Playville Club cuisine is praised by gourm

The famed Prince Ludwig Charmink arriv
the Playville Club looking for a girl to fi
his slippers.

The celebrated Bog Freen is greeted by two admiring Playmooses.

Almost completed -- the Playville Club in Gurneyville, Calif.

Some of the members think that $1.50 a drink is too high.

Some happy Playmooses after a typical "fun" evening!

Another keyholder looking for his club!

Jay Ward
PLAYVILLE CLUBS

Playville Club News

All the while, the wittily acerbic mailers kept coming – an early-60's blitz of promotions aimed primarily at newspaper and magazine columnists, TV and advertising executives, and the like.

Now!!

AT LAST!
A DISCOUNT HOUSE FOR TV SERIES!

BUY AT JAY WARD AND SAVE!!!!

Jay Ward Productions

Yes, Jay Ward Productions is the first to offer quality TV series at low, low discount prices! Up to 40% off!

HOW DOES JAY WARD DO IT?

1. LOW OVERHEAD. No fancy fixtures, no carpeting! Jay Ward films are sold off inexpensive pipe racks. The savings are passed along to you!

2. CHILD LABOR. For years, Jay Ward has found it difficult to imagine why his spendthrift competitors continue to pay high adult wages when there is so much child labor available.

3. OUT OF HIGH RENT DISTRICT. Why have expensive studios in New York and Hollywood? Jay Ward's production facilities are located in an abandoned atomic testing area near Frenchman's Flat, Nevada. Rents here average $ .30 per acre a month. Again, these savings are passed along to you!

4. LESS EXPENSIVE MATERIALS. War surplus stuff, whenever possible. Partially exposed film, retread erasers and short, discardable pencils are carelessly thrown away elsewhere, but are a way of life at Jay Ward Productions.

Animation Dept.

5. NO HIGH-PRICED EXECUTIVES. We all bring our lunches, for instance. And you should see the lunches on these salaries! No Kaiser foil, even; just bread wrappers. A man with actual balogna in his sandwich would be suspected of accepting outside work.

6. NARROW MARGIN OF PROFIT. Jay Ward makes only $40.00 on every series he sells, but makes it up in big-volume sales.

JAY WARD -- THE ROBERT HALL OF SHOW BIZ!!

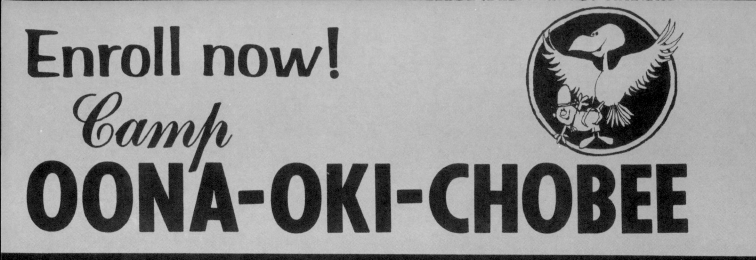

Enroll now!
Camp
OONA-OKI-CHOBEE

Yes! Jay Ward Productions does it again! Imagine — a summer camp for advertising men, sponsors, and TV executives!

Spend 13 carefree weeks away from summer re-runs! Have a B.B.D. & O. account exec for a bunkie! Swim and Indian wrestle with NBC and CBS vice-presidents!

CRAFTS

Make yourself a hand-tooled brief case, a snappy whistle cord, or a clay ash tray for your boss's desk! Jay Ward's patient instructors will show you how.

SEMINARS

"Phrase-Coining"

Jolly Jay Ward writers will help you develop your ability to come up with such snappy sayings as:
"Let's eat the fat and check the cholesterol count later."
COPYRIGHT 1961-JAY WARD PRODS.

"How to Clean Out A Desk in 8 Minutes Flat"

by a former NBC executive

"How to Get A Dozen Series Out Of One Format"

by an ABC programming executive.

RECREATION

Plenty of it! Three hours of Jay Ward pilot films every evening!

TV jingle singing around the campfire!

COUNSELORS:

Courtesy of Vic Tanny, Debbie Drake, Jack LaLanne, and the Playboy Club.

DELICIOUS FOOD!

Nourishing, big TV dinners daily!

An Oona-Oki-Chobee boy

Running it up the flagpole to see who salutes it.

Send these boys to camp!

CAMP Jay T. Ward

NOW!

AT LAST!

A SUMMER CAMP FOR TV EDITORS AND COLUMNISTS!!

CAMP JAY T. WARD

Camp Jay T. Ward, named after the famed TV pioneer and Indian Scout, is located just eighty miles from Chili Burger, Saskatchewan, in an area completely inaccessable to TV!

Think of it! Thirteen glorious weeks away from summer re-runs! More than three months away from "Perry Mason" re-runs and "The Best of Groucho"!

HERE ARE JUST A FEW OF THE EXCITING HIGHLIGHTS OF YOUR SUMMER AT CAMP JAY T. WARD:

1. No daily column to write! Jay Ward Prods. staff of pixie writers will compose your column for you. Seventy-eight (78) complete columns are included in your fee! We promise not to mention Jay Ward Productions more than four times a week. (Ward's writers will also write your letters home for a nominal charge.)

2. Time magazine extension course, conducted by their TV and movie critics, in Advanced Derision, Pun-making, and Elementary Rapier Wit.

3. Seminars on composing snappy answers to Letters-to-the-Editor!

4. Lovely counselors (some of them girls!)

5. Evening campfire singing with Mitch Miller, topped by three full hours of Jay Ward TV pilots, every evening!

As a special offer, generous Jay Ward is offering a special HALF-PRICE fee to any columnist who mentions Jay Ward Productions and/or its TV shows twenty-five (25) times before midnight, June 15, 1961.

Ward

- -

CAMP JAY T. WARD
c/o JAY WARD PRODS.
8218 Sunset Boulevard
Hollywood 46, California

☐ Please send application blank

☐ Please contact my editor

I'd love to but, _____

_____

SIGNED _____

NEWSPAPER _____

If a particular piece of shtick worked once, well, then why not retool a bit and send it right out again?

Dullsville Rest-wise Manor

THE JAY WARD REST HOME FOR ADVERTISING OLD FOLKS!

Ever-thoughtful Jay Ward Productions has done it again! Imagine — a place where the retired advertising man can spend his golden days, in an environment and atmosphere he has grown to love! Who else but Jay Ward would have thought of it?

LOOK AT THESE EXCLUSIVE FEATURES!

1. Dullsville Rest-wise gives you IDENTITY!

2. Each guest is furnished with an executive case of his very own, handy for pills, extra plate, Serutan supply, truss!

3. High-pressure conferences on the hour and lesser meetings every fifteen minutes!

4. The hospital staff is constantly changed and re-shuffled, to provide you with that delicious sensation of insecurity!

5. Drink Dullsville Rest-wise martinis (5 parts mineral oil, 1 part Pepto-Bismol, olive) with the rest of the gang while you think up new catch-phrases like:

   "Let's put this in the wheelchair and see if it rolls to the Social Security Office!"

   "...Speaking off the top of my dentures..."

   "Let's print this on the Geritol bottle and see how they take it!"

WRITE TODAY FOR FURTHER INFORMATION. The first fifty applicants will be sent — without charge — a group photo of Batten, Barton, Durstine, and Osborn, taken during their last coffee-break together.

The mailers were written mostly by Allan Burns and veteran TV comedy writer George Atkins. Burns, drawing on his greeting card experience, did the graphic design and laid most of them out.

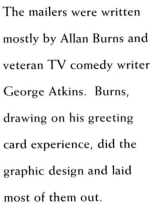

Sarnoff Shopping Center

MODEL HOME

Arbitron Blvd.

JAY WARD'S VIDEO VILLAGE

A DEVELOPMENT OF JAY WARD PRODS.

introducing:

Jay Ward's

VIDEO VILLAGE

Yes! A housing development exclusively for TV folk!

Think of it! Here is an opportunity to rub elbows with ad-men, sponsors, and network executives on an around-the-clock basis! Make frantic lunch-and-cocktail deals a thing of the past! Close a 39-week deal over the back fence! Have a rating war with your next-door-neighbor! Watch the neighborhood children form CBS, ABC and NBC gangs!

These are only a few of the more appealing aspects of living in JAY WARD'S VIDEO VILLAGE!

And. . .only VIDEO VILLAGE offers these deluxe features:

1. *Each home has an intercom system with constant, up-to-the-minute Neilsen's and ARB's!*

2. *Pay-TV exclusively!*

3. *Drive-in theatre for pilot films!*

4. *Individual styling! (Ranch-type houses for ABC programming execs, etc.,*

5. *Short-term leases for NBC employees!*

6. *Veteran's Loans for current Jay Ward Prods. clients!*

JAY WARD PEACE CORPS

Applications are now being taken for those interested in serving in the Jay Ward Peace Corps, an organization dedicated to putting out the Jay Ward Productions message to underdeveloped ad agencies and sponsors throughout the free world. Since the formation of the Jay Ward Peace Corps was first announced, three applications have poured in from all parts of the country. This daring innovation has fired the imagination of all America.

"...Our Peace Corps members will work 16 hours a day if necessary...without compensation of any kind. Their lives will not be easy — they must endure the same standard of living as that of those with whom they will work — even if that is an agency with billings of only $20 million a year! Their only reward will be the satisfaction of knowing they have helped to sell Jay Ward Productions to the world!"

—— Jay Ward
March 23, 1961

These stirring words have already inspired many to act. How about you? Write today for further information.

(NOTE: Service in the Jay Ward Peace Corps does not mean exemption from military duty.)

Here's what some famous Americans have to say about the Jay Ward Peace Corps:

Eleanor Roosevelt —— "Jay WHO?!"

Dean Rusk —— "Huh?!"

Richard M. Nixon —— "I am making a study of the matter and I will make a statement at a later date."

Bernard Baruch —— "Who is Jay Ward?"

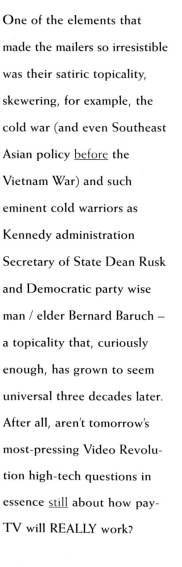

One of the elements that made the mailers so irresistible was their satiric topicality, skewering, for example, the cold war (and even Southeast Asian policy _before_ the Vietnam War) and such eminent cold warriors as Kennedy administration Secretary of State Dean Rusk and Democratic party wise man / elder Bernard Baruch — a topicality that, curiously enough, has grown to seem universal three decades later. After all, aren't tomorrow's most-pressing Video Revolution high-tech questions in essence _still_ about how pay-TV will REALLY work?

How will pay-tv REALLY work?

Have you wondered too? We have, and we've come up with a really wonderful way to find out how you like pay television and if you'd like to have more of it!

HERE'S ALL YOU DO:

First, watch the exciting new "BULLWINKLE SHOW" every Sunday evening on NBC (in color).

Next, after each show you simply mail the producers of the "BULLWINKLE SHOW" some money so that you can get the feel of pay-TV. *

Then, we'll write you back and tell you how it feels to get money from pay-TV.

Simple? Easy? You bet!

What do you say we try it ! **

> **JAY WARD PRODUCTIONS**
> 8218 Sunset Boulevard
> Hollywood 46, California

* Please do not mention this to anybody at NBC because they probably wouldn't like it at all.

** Please do not show this circular to any FCC people, as we haven't mentioned it to them yet.

The BULLWINKLE Show

There was always opposition from the network, says Brandy. "There was never smooth sailing."

And Ramona Ward remembers business trips her husband would take, "trips to New York. He'd have all the appointments set up [with network programming executives] before he got there and they'd call and not see him. He'd sit there for days and he'd [phone and] say, 'I cannot come home yet, I haven't seen these people, I haven't done this or that.' It was very difficult. Oh, they'd sit there and laugh and laugh and laugh [but] they didn't get it."

In the spirit of the dotty admiral that he presented himself as, though, Jay Ward kept the writers blissfully unaware of the network's pressures and the show's precariousness. "You never heard from Jay, 'Couldn't we please somebody, couldn't we change this a little bit to please somebody'" recalls writer/producer Burns. "He'd always say, 'To hell with those guys! I hate them! Let's just do it.' And then he'd fight those battles.... Of course, I only heard about this later."

(Ramona Ward disputes this recollection for a very particular reason: "I knew Jay Ward for fifty years and I never heard him use the word 'hell,' or any other swear word for that matter," she says adamantly.)

However, by the fall season 'sixty-two premiere mailer, headlined *Thanks Anyhow...*, the strain underneath the humor clearly sounds.

THANKS
ANYHOW...

We are aware that there are many of you who have been anxiously waiting to help us publicize the beginning of our second season on NBC.   We imagine there are many columnists holding two weeks of space open, ready to dazzle their readers with Bullwinkle goodies when the time comes, as well as those "Bullwinkle's Back!" rallies planned for Madison Square Garden and the Cow Palace. We've heard there are telethon organizers and chain letter writers waiting on their marks for our slightest word.

As much as we're moved by your loyalty and enthusiasm for our modest offering, we must ask you to cancel those plans. Please devote your energies toward promoting those shows which are needier than ours – "Ben Casey", "Wagon Train", "Dr. Kildare", "Ed Sullivan". Therefore, instead of the reams of promotional material with which we showered you prior to last year's air date, this year we are simply sending you this one lone mailer.

Furthermore, we have no plans to herald this season's premiere with a black-tie, 10 highball, 12 searchlight affair like last year's. We feel that this might be interpreted as a somewhat ostentatious display, in view of the heavy casualty rate among last year's cartoon shows. Instead, Mr. Ward will be on the front steps of our little studio with a flashlight, dispensing rum candies to those of you who'd like to drop by and catch the show on his portable TV.

The great mailer campaign of 1961 was focused particularly on calling attention to Rocky and Bullwinkle's move from ABC to NBC, a network with whom Jay Ward seemed forever after at war. They might have played that for laughs in the mailers – in the same way that David Letterman used to call NBC executives pinheads before defecting to CBS – but behind the scenes it was really no laughing matter.

On air and off, the Wardsters irritated the network. Not only did Bullwinkle once blithely advise home viewers to rip the channel-changing knobs from their sets (to better tune in the following week, of course), but one mailer – the infamous Color Correction Kit – offered a "sheet of scientifically treated cellophane to receive *The Bullwinkle Show* in sharp, vivid black and white. Watch it in black and white, as more unfortunate people must."

NBC's corporate parent, RCA, proud maker of the color TV sets that it was just then introducing to an avid populace, was not amused.

COLOR SET OWNERS!

Here it is!

WHAT YOU'VE BEEN WAITING FOR!!

JayWardProductions
COLOR CORRECTION KIT

Simply tape this sheet of scientifically treated cellophane over your color tube to receive "The Bullwinkle Show" in sharp, vivid black and white! Mask out those lush, vibrant colors that merely add to your enjoyment. Watch it in black and white, as more unfortunate people must.

WHY?

First, what could be more democratic? After all, many people don't have color sets. Why antagonize them because they can't enjoy the full richness of "The Bullwinkle Show" on their crummy black and white sets? Our COLOR CORRECTION KIT solves this ticklish problem for you.

Second, black and white TV is quaint, charming —— like Roaring 20's bars, silent movies, and wind-up Victorolas. As a matter of fact, you might mask off your TV screen entirely and just listen to "The Bullwinkle Show". Just like radio! With ear-phones, even!

Go ahead —— try it! We think you'll be glad you caught "The Bullwinkle Show" in this exciting new process.

THE BULLWINKLE SHOW   SUNDAY EVENINGS ON NBC-TV   IN COLOR

The remarkable
GROVER S. TWEET
says:

GROVER S. TWEET

"I predict that the new Bullwinkle Show will be the popular and critical sensation of the 1961-62 television season. It will undoubtedly win an Emmy, for it has everything: hilarious comedy, satire, color, action, adventure, and universality of appeal. It just can't miss!!"

Other Grover S. Tweet quotes:

"The economic structure of the United States has never been more sound." (Oct. 1, 1929)

"...We here at the Literary Digest are betting everything on a Landon victory!" (Nov. 3, 1936)

"America only has one true friend on which to depend and that is the Empire of Japan." (Dec. 6, 1941)

"I wholeheartedly support a Cuban invasion because it cannot possibly fail. Superior forces, arms, and air support on our side, and anyway, the Cuban people loathe Castro!"

THE BULLWINKLE SHOW · NBC · SUNDAYS

where will you be on

sunday evening
sept. 24?

If you are Winnie Ruth Judd, you will hold off that escape attempt for thirty minutes while you go into the day-room with the rest of the prisoners to watch the premiere of "The Bullwinkle Show".

If you are "Lucky" Luciano, you will smash your fist through a priceless Botticelli in your palatial Naples home in anger and frustration — because you can't see the new "Bullwinkle Show" in Italy.

If you are Alf Landon, you will consider sending of wire of bestwishes to the producers of "The Bullwinkle Show", but then decide against it, as it might be misinterpreted as a comeback try.

If you are Mrs. Florence Aadland, you will put aside your almost-completed manuscript of "Dr. Spock of the Teenage World" and switch on "The Bullwinkle Show" on your new color set, a gift from Parents' Magazine.

If you are Joe Kennedy, you will call the kids in from their touch football game in time to catch "The Bullwinkle Show".

If you are the producers of the show, you will be booking passage on a tramp steamer with an 11,000 mile destination. You leave no forwarding address, no notes. You look frightened.

BULLWINKLE

NBC

HERE IT IS!

BULLWINKLE J. MOOSE
Protection Card

Bullwinkle J. Moose

The closest thing to complete police protection available!
It's your BULLWINKLE PROTECTION CARD.

That's right. Jay Ward has made deals with police departments all over the United States, so that when you see those flashing red lights and hear that siren you can feel secure. When the officer approaches your car with that "Going to a fire?" expression, simply flash your BULLWINKLE PROTECTION CARD and it's all over in seconds!

TRY IT!

Notice that policeman's change of attitude when he sees that card. Remember, he's used to seeing drivers nervously fumbling for their licenses. When he sees you coolly and suavely going for a small picture of a stupid moose –– well, sir, he's going to be impressed. We'll bet you'll get a reaction like you've never gotten from a cop before.

Why have we gone to all this trouble? It's just a small gesture to promote our new "Bullwinkle Show", Sunday evenings on NBC-TV. In Color.

NOTE: Should anything go wrong, please do not contact us, but perhaps the warden may give you recreation room privileges so that you can catch the show each Sunday.

It's not just the words that people remember. There's Rocky and Bullwinkle's simple but oddly stylish look too. ❧ It was, fittingly enough, the incongruously happy result of necessity and serendipity. The naive Mexican animation, the rapid shock cuts, the perpetually

reused in-between and background drawings — somehow, synergistically, the result looks just *fine*.

One authority in the animation-as-art field even goes so far as to say that Rocky and Bullwinkle's literary references, exuberant wordplay, and shameless show-biz shtick wouldn't play as well if done in a more painterly animation style.

"If you took Rocky and Bullwinkle, the gags, and put it together with fine, full, feature animation like Disney could do, it wouldn't work," says Ron Stark, the director and cofounder of S/R Laboratories, an animation-art center created originally as a project of the International Animated Film Society. "The look fits, even though it's unsophisticated....

"It's visually irreverent. In an artistic sense, it's as witty as the writing because it doesn't give you anything to focus on," he says, citing as an example background buildings drawn "much like a kid would draw them, with the sides showing in front."

What Jay Ward, Bill Scott, Bill Hurtz, and the others responsible for the animation look were "trying to convey," Stark adds, "is:...don't distract the eye from the humor that's in the [audio] track; make it as off center as you can and still retain the visual pleasing-ness of the show."

At Disney, the house of classically beautiful animation, "they" "despised, just loathed" that simple Ward style, recalls director Bill Hurtz. It was true at Hanna-Barbera, Warner, and most of the other animation shops around Hollywood too, according to Hurtz, where the Ward style was looked down on as "just [cheap] TV," and the Wardsters themselves, however brilliant, were considered just a band of mavericks and misfits, most of whom had learned their craft at equally iconoclastic UPA, the Oscar-winning production home of such stylish departures as *Mr. Magoo* and *Gerald McBoing-Boing*.

Ward liked animation "with an edge," writer Allan Burns says, and that attracted him to the UPA animators and other disaffected creative types. "Most of the guys who worked for [Ward] were former Disney guys who...didn't like that kind of stuff and had drifted away to places like Warner Bros., where they were at least doing *Looney Tunes*, which were pretty funny. The guys who found that a little stifling...went along to places like UPA, where they were working on avant garde animation at least.

"Then a lot of them were offended by a guy...who owned UPA, who was sort of an Attila the Hun with all these creative people...Jay was the recipient of a lot of that talent eventually."

By all accounts, it wasn't just Disneyites who looked down on Ward. Disney animation was "boring as far as [Jay] was concerned," says Burns. "On the other hand, there may have been a sort of jealousy of the beauty of the animation. He was never able to afford that stuff."

Jay Ward "admired [Disney] for what he achieved," says Ron Ward, the elder of his two sons. But the Disney style "wasn't particularly his kind of humor or his kind of animation."

And, of course, the Studio the Mouse Built made an irresistible satirical target. That satire turned up most famously in two "Fractured Fairy Tales," but early on in the show's run – when NBC was using its weekly *Wonderful World of Color* series from Disney to push all those newfangled color TV sets that parent company RCA was then first cranking out, with Donald Duck and Professor Ludwig Von

Drake enlisted as prominent color-TV spokesbirds – Ward got off a double-barreled blast, bringing out Bullwinkle to explain how the benighted still-watching-in-black-and-white viewing audience could visualize the wonderful world of color: "Its really very easy," the moose explained. "First, think of your income tax. Next, Mr. Khrushchev's latest [Commie Red Menace] speech. Then think about what Mr. Disney said about your [obsolete] black-and-white set....Makes you see red, doesn't it?" Reportedly, neither the network nor Disney was amused.

In "The Ugly Almond Duckling," one of the two classic Disney-baiting "Fractured Fairy Tales," Edward Everett Horton, the acerbic-tongued character actor who was a frequent foil in thirties Fred Astaire-Ginger Rogers musicals (and at the time of the recording sessions was an octogenarian conveyed to and fro in a Rolls Royce limousine), relates deadpan the tale of a Chinese duck who lives by the Yangtze River (you know, the waterway that inspired the song, "Yangtze with the Laughing Face"?).

Of course, like his fellow honkers, this extremely ugly duck desires nothing more than to be selected for the emperor's favorite dish, almond duckling. But the ugliest duckling is banished from the pond instead, so he sets off to get talented, hoping that perhaps, someday, the cook will select him.

The determined duckling studies night and day (and other songs too) at the Rock and Egg Roll Conservatory of Music and, after an entire year, he's mastered an amazing array of musical instruments, but, instead of being selected for dinner, he's willy-nilly turned into a show business sensation who's represented by mega-agency MCA (an actual company, now corporate parent of Universal Pictures).

Still, all he wants to do is be served – for the Emperor's dinner, that is – until one day, through the power of positive thinking, he transforms himself into the handsomest duck in the entire pond, and he's selected after all – but not by the cook, for you see, this duck's name is Donald, and a man named Walt has put him to work...as a quacky daffy duck.

Although we only see his back, "Walt" is clearly Walt Disney. He's even more unmistakable in the other "Fairy Tale," the mercantile, Hollywood version of "Sleeping Beauty," in which the prince has the fast-talking, Bronx-accented voice of fifties TV con-artist-in-uniform Sergeant

Bilko (veteran second banana Phil Silvers), but looks just like Uncle Walt, right down to his pencil-thin moustache.

This prince doesn't wake Sleeping Beauty – that would interfere with *his* dream: *"I can see it now: Sleeping Beauty comics! Sleeping Beauty hats! Sleeping Beauty bubble gum! And biggest of all...Sleeping Beauty Land!"*

Soon, the castle's become a tourist attraction and there's a *Variety*-ese headline in the show biz trades: *Doze Doll Duz Wiz Biz!* Eventually, though, something astounding happens: the princess awakens, without even the need of a kiss! "Don't worry, kids," she says breezily, "I wasn't really asleep....I just wanted to see if I could make it in show biz!"

Ironically, given how often and with what obvious glee the Wardsters tweaked the Master of the Mouse, in the late eighties the heirs to the Magic Kingdom bought video rights to "Rocky and Bullwinkle," selling almost

two million tapes at almost thirteen bucks each in the first month of release alone. Yet, to this day, Allan Burns and Skip Craig, Wardsters at heart still, find themselves amazed to be, respectively, ensconced as a writer/producer on the Disney lot and an animation editor in Disney's employ.

In the bull (moose) animation-art market of the eighties, though, when there was nothing Mickey Mouse about what Mickey was selling for at the likes of Sotheby's, the value of Rocky and Bullwinkle animation, original and otherwise, was rocketing into the stratosphere too. In fact, says animation-art expert Stark, rumors of a cache of original Rocky and Bullwinkle art hidden in a Mexican cave have circulated for years.

Maybe the treasure of the Sierra Madre will turn out to be a cartoon moose and cartoon flying squirrel. *Who knew the stuff was valuable?* is a refrain constantly sounded by veterans of those late-fifties/early-sixties days. In fact, one-time Jay Ward secretary Linda Simmons Hayward confesses cheerfully to disposing of a veritable treasure trove of animation art herself.

"I'll tell you, I knew so little that I'm the one that threw out all the film," she says of the original animation cells cluttering up the crowded office. "[Jay] would just pile them in the room and I would say, 'I can't stand this, I'm a clean nut. How could you let this go?' I'd go in and say, 'This is cleaning day' and come in in jeans — it

wasn't jeans in those days, it was probably the shortest skirt I could find — and I would go in and throw stuff away, and [Jay] would laugh every time....The place was such a mess. I should have just left it that way. That would have been the smart thing."

Financially smart, anyway. But then again, back then, *who knew?*

Over the years of the financially mandated and always dreaded Mexican animation, from episode to episode Bullwinkle's color would change slightly or his mouth might not move in concert with Bill Scott's spoken works on the audio track. Viewers and critics alike may have hailed the sophistication of adult dialogue combined with childlike drawing, but the inconsistencies drove Jay Ward and company wild.

"The simplicity and the stylishness really came from necessity," says the man who set up the Mexican studio that the sponsor mandated and who had to work with the inexperienced freelance animators there. "We didn't have the money to fool around."

As time went on, though, the young, inexperienced Mexican animators, who were paid "practically nothing," according to Bill Hurtz, mastered the skills of drawing Rocky, Bullwinkle, and friends the way they were *supposed* to look.

Like many other reigning cultural icons, Bullwinkle J. Moose now faces the future after a slight but state-of-the-art makeover. "With [the help of] artistic people, we have kind of updated Bullwinkle's look," says the managing director of Jay Ward Productions, his daughter, Tiffany. "Rocky hasn't changed, but Bullwinkle, with Mother's and my permission, has....His nose is less long and angular; it's rounder. We've perked up the colors a little bit; [it's] more nineties-looking....

"Actually, if you really study the [films] from 'fifty-nine to 'sixty-four, he changed a lot in that period of time, so we just kind of improved him, [to] where he looks a little more hip."

Bullwinkle <u>more</u> hip? Why, ever since the late fifties, hasn't the debonair B.J. Moose <u>defined</u> hip?

By the time of Bullwinkle's only solo guest-star turn – nothing less than a live-action-married-with-animation song-and-dance number with crooner Vic Damone, on the premiere of NBC's short-lived, summer-replacement, musical-variety series <u>The Lively Ones</u> – the look was fixed. There were no computers megabyting out special effects then, and using the blue-screen process on TV to combine actors and cartoon characters was still fairly new. Typically, the Wardsters approached the technically daunting project in a spirit of improvisation and under a tight deadline. The singer's choreographer was simply brought out to direct Bill Hurtz's San Fernando Valley home one fine day, a 16-mm camera was set up in the shady yard, and he was filmed tripping through the moves to an audiotape playback on the back patio, which was chalked off in a grid for the occasion. Later, three animators worked around the clock, copying the choreographer's every move frame by frame off an ancient Movieola, to animate the big terpsichorean moose in time for the show's fast-approaching airdate.

There are three hundred and twenty-six individual Rocky and Bullwinkle episodes, each three and a half minutes long.

The twenty-eight stories they comprise begin with the forty-episode "Jet Fuel Formula," in which our heroes discover a new rocket fuel made from mooseberries and do battle with both pixilated moon men and bumbling Pottsylvanian spies, and end with the four-episode "Moosylvania Saved," in which Rocky and Bullwinkle prevent their island homeland from sinking under the weight of erroneously sent American foreign aid.

From the first episode (in which Grandma Bullwinkle's fudge cake recipe turns out to be a revolutionary rocket fuel and Bullwinkle is named Director of Guided Moosles) to last (in which U.S. government aid almost sinks the island of Moosylvania), bumbling bureaucrats and venal politicians are frequent satirical targets, as are the conventions of show business itself.

Synopses follow. Read them the way Jay Ward always urged narrator William Conrad to read *his* lines: Faster. Faster! *Faster!*

JET FUEL FORMULA

EPISODES 1–40

WHILE BAKING GRANDMA BULLWINKLE'S EXPLOSIVE RECIPE

for delicious mooseberry-flavored fudge cake, Rocky and Bullwinkle inadvertently discover a fantastic new rocket fuel that propels them to the moon and back. Bullwinkle is immediately made Director of Guided Moosles.

Two

Because the recipe had been torn apart in the explosion, Bullwinkle knows how much but not what of, so he and Rocky set to work in their government laboratory, while at universities all over the country cake baking is being added to the scientific curriculum. Meanwhile, after failing in an attempt to time-bomb the Moose, Boris and

Natasha do what any intelligent, self-sufficient spies with real initiative would do: They wait for instructions!

Three

Those little green men holding extremely ominous-looking weapons aren't congressmen, as Bullwinkle first surmises, they're Gidney and Cloyd, reluctant visitors from the moon, here to keep an invasion of earth tourists from cluttering up their homeland. Indeed, just to prepare for their visit, the two have had to practice dodging traffic, listening to jukeboxes, filling out forms, and breathing smog! Meanwhile, Boris and Natasha, twelve stories up with a heavy safe as our heroes stroll by below, finally receive orders from headquarters: KILL MOOSE!

Four

Whoops. The actual orders said *DON'T* KILL MOOSE, so Boris races the safe to keep Bullwinkle safe, and it's safe to say he *almost* makes it. It's back to the laboratory for our heroes, where they turn out acres of cinnamon pizzas and hot fudge strudels, but none of it's explosive. Just as Rocky's thinking hypnotism might be something to try, Swami Ben Boris and

his assistant appear, putting Bullwinkle into a trance and, forthwith, the moose tells *everything* he knows – all about his early years in the Minnesota woods, his days at the Philpott School for Exceptional Children (he was the only student with antlers), his experiences in the army, where for three years he served as a hat rack in the Officers' Club – going on and on for a full twelve hours and boring everyone within hearing distance into dreamland, so that when he finally gets to the part about the recipe, the only ones awake to hear it are the two moon men. Forthwith, Cloyd raises his weapon and scrooches the big moose!

Five

The scrooch gun has frozen Bullwinkle solid, and Cloyd and Gidney start off with their moosesicle as a trophy of their visit to a small planet, but Boris comes to in time to con them into leaving Moose for him, while they get Squirrel, the brains of the operation. While the moon men are telling Rocky they can't remember if they've scrooched Bullwinkle for eight hours or eight years...WHISK! Eight hours later, Bullwinkle thaws out in Boris's laboratory, where every word he says is monitored in another country by a faraway band of ominous spies.

Six

Every move the moose makes is duplicated in the faraway spy lab. Bullwinkle cooks up some tasty chocolate pan dowdy that blows up when the spies try it, and when Rocky smells the delicious aroma, it leads him right to Bullwinkle, but Boris is ready with a helpful trapdoor that sends the plucky squirrel falling into another stew!

Seven

Rocky's blown away all right, drifting out to sea in a leaky hot air ballon courtesy of Boris Badenov.

Meanwhile, an anxious nation and two anxious moon men are searching for the missing moose, who's still baking away in Boris's secret laboratory. By going door-to-door to every house in the country, Gidney and Cloyd eventually turn up there, so Boris and Natasha quickly throw them a surprise party complete with knockout punch, while back out over the stormy seas, lightning strikes Rocky's balloon, sending it plunging.

Eight

Fortunately, Bullwinkle offers the wrong toast – "To crime!" – and Boris and Natasha, official bad guys that they are, are obliged to drink up, gulping down their own knockout punch; meanwhile, the flying squirrel is being used for target practice by the U.S. Navy, until quick-witted Rocky uses the smoke from the antiaircraft fire to spell out the phrase: *U.S. TAXPAYER* – and, of course, the navy needs every one of those that it can get. Soon Rocky finds Bullwinkle, and just as our heroes are about to leave with the moon men, a grateful U.S. government responds by arresting them!

Nine

Yes, the government agents who've arrested our heroes are hunting for two spies. If it's not Rocky and Bullwinkle, it must be those two funny-looking green guys, reasons Special Agent Iris T. Upthecreek, but when he tries to take the moon men into custody, he's scrooched...for a full fifty years, which creates a tiny problem until Rocket J. hits upon the idea of putting the scrooched agent on a pedestal, right in front of the National Security Building, while he slowly thaws. Meanwhile, the moon men have become media darlings, with pointed heads all the rage, and they're even given the keys to the city (they're delicious). Cloyd and Gidney respond to all this flattering attention by heading back to their spaceship for a little peace and quiet, but ensuring that same peace and quiet on the moon means

keeping Grandma Moose's recipe out of earthling hands, so it looks as if our heroes are going to be forced to go lunar themselves.

Ten

Up and up they go, and then down and down: Cloyd and Gidney are out of fuel, or is that fudge cake? Because Boris and Natasha have absconded with their last fuel tank, the moon men have no choice but to tell Rocky the recipe, and they're just one ingredient short: mooseberry juice, which grows in only one place in the entire nation, and that hard-to-find spot just happens to be Rocky and Bullwinkle's hometown, *Frostbite Falls, Minnesota* (population twenty-three). Meanwhile, Boris and Natasha, those two creeps in the deep, board a midget submarine.

Eleven

Boris has plenty of medals – for burning down orphanages, for kicking small dogs, for taking candy from babies – so why isn't he happier? He's forgotten something, he's certain, but can't remember what it is until he gets his orders: KILL MOOSE! So, of course, he and Natasha put the

sub on autopilot, slip into breathing apparatus, and swim straight back to the U.S. of A. Meanwhile, our heroes are finding it tough to get to Frostbite Falls, so they head off to the nearest airfield to rent a cut-rate private plane, where they immediately find Ace Ricken-Boris, whose motto is *Fly Now, Pray Later*. Rocky wants to do some square business, but all Ace Ricken-Boris is offering are round trips for eighty-five cents per, which just happens to be all the money Rocky and Bullwinkle have. Is Ace really wild about flying them to Frostbite Falls, dollink, or is that vaguely familiar, vampy stewardess strapping our heroes into a flying casket?

Twelve

The auto-controlled spy sub goes slightly out of control, blowing up an entire foreign port. Meanwhile, after fastening Rocky and Bullwinkle into one-way seat belts, stewardess Natasha bails out, while Boris gleefully smashes instruments in the pilot's compartment. It looks like a smash landing ahead.

Thirteen

A last-second reconsideration of orders from headquarters (the message didn't say KILL MOOSE; it actually read DON'T KILL MOOSE) means Boris has to save Rocky and Bullwinkle, whose brilliant idea to retrieve the last mooseberry bush on

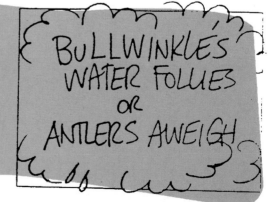

Mooseberry Island (SWIM THE RIVER!) has one tiny flaw (Bullwinkle doesn't know how to swim!).

Fourteen

Despite going over Thundering Falls, Bullwinkle, by remaining cuke as a coolcumber, manages to snatch the last available mooseberry bush in the entire country, but a federal plant inspector with a familiar accent turns up, spraying the precious bush for blight, and forthwith, he and the bush disappear behind the huge cloud.

Fifteen

Those laughing Indians going by in a canoe aren't part of the Minnie-Ho-Ho tribe, but really Boris and Natasha with the purloined plant, so the big canoe race is on, with our heroes transforming their crashed plane into a water-worthy craft.

Sixteen

From Frostbite Falls, it's across a couple of the Great Lakes and portage through downtown Chicago, as the Great Canoe and Leaky Retrofitted Airplane Race is on! It's stroke–stroke–stroke and bail–bail–bail as the pursuit continues down ever more tiny waterways! And finally on one foggy evening, as they approach Washington, D.C., the two competing vessels are so close that – stroke–bail, bail–stroke – their echoes are even writing their own dialogue! But our heroes, prompted by some dastardly sign rewriting, take the wrong turn, heading directly toward the hideously whirling blade of a sawmill just ahead. Will it be Two for the Ripsaw, or, is it Good-bye, Mister Chips?

Seventeen

It's getting choppy out there all right, but even though the whirling blade cuts their little vessel in two, our heroes escape unscathed because… they're sitting on opposite sides of the craft! Rocky and Bullwinkle return to their laboratory in something less than triumph, booed by the fickle citizenry just because they've lost the mooseberry bush, while Boris and Natasha get ready to set sail for their homeland.

Eighteen

If only they knew the whereabouts of another mooseberry bush! Perhaps the moon men will tell them, but when our heroes go to New York to call on Gidney and Cloyd, all they find is a theatrical newspaper with the headline: MOON MEN SOCKO IN LOS WAGES! BOFFO B.O.! Sure enough, Bullwinkle baby, the moon men have gone Hollywood, but they take time out from taking bows to take a long-distance call backstage

and clue the moose in: There's a mooseberry bush to be found in Pottsylvania, a menacing little land that just happens to be where Boris and Natasha are from!

Nineteen

Rocky and Bullwinkle are up to their necks in trouble…and in water too, for Boris Badenov has dumped them into the harbor and a huge ocean liner is bearing down on them, about to squeeze them against the dock!

Twenty

Picked up by the mighty S.S. *Andalusia,* plowing her way through the seas to Pottsylvania, Bullwinkle sits basking on deck next to a taciturn old gentleman, Sir Thomas Lippen-Boris – Uncle Chumley, actually – the purloined mooseberry bush in disguise! Meanwhile, Boris is boring…holes in a lifeboat, that is.

Twenty-one

Tricked by a fake lifeboat drill called by Boris Badenov, that dastardly USC graduate (that is, the Ukrainian Safecracking College, dollink), into a leaky lifeboat – Moose overboard! – our heroes are all at sea and lost in a fog. But little does Boris know that Moose and Squirrel have courteously taken along that old and taciturn (and red and green and spotted) gentleman, Uncle Chumley, who bears an uncanny resemblance to a certain mooseberry bush.

Twenty-two

Bullwinkle has a sinking feeling that their boat is leaking, but when Rocky has Bullwinkle stand on his head, the points of his antlers fit exactly the holes in the boat! Unfortunately, the S.S. *Andalusia* – commanded by none other than Captain Peter "Wrong Way" Peachfuzz, recipient of a plethora of medals, all of them bestowed by the enemy – bears directly down on our heroes! Will it be the Deep Six, or, is it The Old Moose and the Sea?

Twenty-three

There's nothing but splinters left of the little lifeboat, but mighty Bullwinkle has managed to grab ahold of the passing anchor, and Rocky has ahold of him, and when Boris looks out his porthole and sees that they have ahold of Uncle Chumley, he has no choice but to grab ahold of our heroes and haul them in. At that moment Captain Peachfuzz veers off again, traveling more miles and getting to fewer places than any other vessel on earth. The captain's outrageous all right, and what's more, the food's almost gone!

Twenty-four

Our heroes are so hungry, they're eating *pictures* of food; meanwhile, Boris and Natasha go picking mooseberries. But when Captain Peachfuzz suddenly veers, Bullwinkle accidentally chomps down a few mooseberries, turning into a living, hiccoughing bomb. Then, hearing the false story that his little friend Rocky has fallen overboard, the big-hearted moose dashes through the door, trips, and hurtles directly toward the deck thirty feet below! It looks like Bullwinkle Makes a Hit, or, Will I Get a Bang out of You?

Twenty-five

It's good news/bad news for Bullwinkle: Fortunately, he's fallen directly into the ship's pool; unfortunately, he can't swim and there's…AN EXPLOSION! But fortunately, it blows all the water out of the pool, leaving Bullwinkle high and dry and feeling just fine, except for a touch of a stomachache. Meanwhile, the wrong-headed captain sets them aground on tropical Baloney Isle, from where Boris and Natasha promptly hijack the ship. There's no one to complain to when it's Three on an Island, or, Go Tell It to the Maroons!

Twenty-six

A native's selling poi burgers, but our hungry heroes aren't biting, because the native won't accept anything (not even Rocky's glow-in-the-dark yo-yo) but the local currency, clams, so Rocky and Bullwinkle have no choice but to go clam digging on the beach, where they spot the S.S. *Andalusia* and Sir Thomas Lippen-Boris, who yet again is under orders to RETURN MOOSE!

Twenty-seven

The good citizens of Pottsylvania have extended our heroes a real Pottsylvanian welcome, for millionaire yachtsman Sir Thomas Lippen-Boris and Lady Alice have prudently disguised Rocky and Bullwinkle as…Boris and Natasha! And under orders from Central Control, the populace is waiting at the dock with open arms – as well as arms of all other kinds, everything from knives and blunderbusses to automatic weapons! The alarmed populace hustles them toward a sinister platform where a hooded executioner waits…and

it's not the keys to the city he's holding! But Axe No Questions, or, It's Heads You Lose!

Twenty-eight

Back in Central Control, Fearless Leader's getting ready to fill Boris's alibi for not having the rocket fuel full of holes. Meanwhile, the Pottsylvanians realize their mistake and generously compensate our heroes for their near execution by throwing them right into jail!

Twenty-nine

The number-one American tourist destination in Pottsylvania turns out to be…jail. The travel folders may have said "Welcome to Pottsylvania," but our heroes have had nothing but trouble since they arrived. First an angry mob, then a near execution, and now it's to jail, where Rocky and Bullwinkle find the tourists and even the American consul. Meanwhile, Fearless Leader reveals his Fiendish Plan to conquer the moon and beam Pottsylvanian TV into the U.S. ("Gritty, grimy, greasy goo, that's what's in our new shampoo. GUNK! Get some today!"), and that requires freeing Moose, so soon lawyer Clarence Darrownoff shows up, but Rocky insists he bail out all the other Americans, who immediately board the S.S. *Andalusia* and, under Captain Peachfuzz's erratic command, they go zigzagging away.

Thirty

Our heroes feel like heroes again, having saved a boatload of tourists, but all is not well yet, because they're stuck in Pottsylvania, the land where *all* the people are spies and everything is a secret! And they don't even like baseball players, Bullwinkle observes with some disbelief when he sees the YANKEE GO HOME signs. But there's no time to speculate, for they must mount the Great

"If you can't believe what you read in comic books, what can you believe?"

Mooseberry Expedition, but it's going to be harder than ever because their hotel room has been burgled and the thieves have made off with everything, including all the money and Bullwinkle's autographed picture of Sonny Tufts!

Thirty-one

Our heroes are closing in at last on the missing mooseberry bush, for they've hired a famous mountain climber with a vaguely familiar face, Sir Hillary Pushemoff, and his friend, the Indian princess Bubbles, to guide them up the Grimalaya mountains to the thirty-two-thousand-foot Whynchataka Peak. From that elevated elevation, surely they can see even the Isle

of Lucy on Veronica Lake!

Thirty-two

Triumph is fleeting in the search for the mooseberry bush, and so is the rapidly growing piece of candy that Boris is rolling down the mountainside directly toward Rocky and Bullwinkle as Princess Bubbles makes off with the bitterly contested bush. Surviving the avalanche, our heroes start off through the snow fields.

Thirty-three

A nice lunch on an overhanging snow ledge

courtesy of Boris Badenov goes from bad to worse when Bullwinkle puts too much pepper on his hard-boiled egg and sneezes the entire ledge off into the abyss. But, believing our heroes are still in possession of the prize bush, Boris digs them out.

Thirty-four

Rocky and Bullwinkle's epic quest and grand dream of converting the rare juice of the magic mooseberry into rocket fuel turns to nightmare when they meet that legendary figure of mountain lore, the dread Abominable Snowman.

Thirty-five

Bullwinkle draws a pole-vault-sized straw when Sir Hillary suggests they draw for the honor of staying

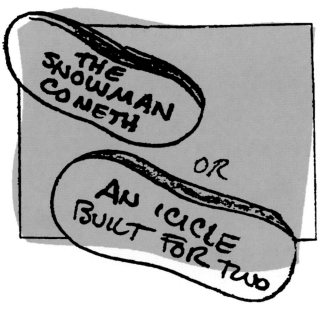

behind and battling the approaching Snowman, but it's Rocky to the rescue! The plucky squirrel hurls himself from a nearby cliff and fearlessly dives straight into the fearsome creature! When the dazed Snowman finally speaks, though, it's not with forked tongue, but two voices...and both voices belong to Cloyd and Gidney! Are the Moon Men Blue or is it to be The Inside Story?

Thirty-six

Boris and Natasha take off in terror, but, unzipped, the menacing Snowman turns out to be two moon men in disguise. After their great show business success, they explain, the two were signed to do a TV western, *Moonsmoke,* but when Marshall Cloyd inadvertently drew his scrooch gun and fired into the camera, the entire home audience was glued to their seats, so naturally the moon men were canceled in favor of beaming round-the-clock commercials at their captive audience. Now that our heroes finally have a mooseberry bush, will Rocky do his duty to his government, or will he let the homesick moon men use it to get back to their home crater?

Thirty-seven

Boris may be a liar, turncoat, and double-crosser, but he's not forgetful, so when he tells Fearless Leader that Moose and Squirrel are kaput it must be true, only just then our heroes turn up, ruining Boris's perfect lie. Now all Rocky and Bullwinkle have to do is get back to the U.S. of A. with the moon men, but it seems everyone in Pottsylvania wants out too, and they're all ahead in a mile-long line. Will it be the Pottsylvania Permanent, and will they Grow Accustomed to the Place?

Thirty-eight

A fortuitous cab from the Tick Tock Taxi Company appears, but it's Boris and Natasha in the driver's seat and TNT under the backseat. When the drivers take a powder, Bullwinkle astutely realizes that the ticking sound he hears must be the taxi meter, so, when he can't find it to turn it off, he, Rocky, and the moon men all get out to explore, but the unattended cab rolls backward down the hill and…BOOM! Fortunately, our heroes have already gotten to the border and they spot a friendly guard nearby, who immediately gets them in his rifle sights. Will they be The Boundary Bounders, or do Some Like It Shot?

Thirty-nine

Cloyd the moon man scrooches the border guard, and our heroes escape on a small freighter to Washington, D.C., where Rocky puts his clever plan for helping the moon men into effect: Because the American government wants the rocket fuel to send an American to the moon, if they make Gidney and Cloyd American citizens, then *they* can travel to the moon. But just then Senator Fussmussen is holding a press conference, announcing his determination to make it *harder* to become a citizen. Will Rocky go into his Washington Whirl, or is Rocky off the Record?

Forty

With Alaskans, Hawaiians, and even Californians claiming to be U.S. citizens, Senator Fussmussen of the Congressional Citizenship Committee takes a stand! So our heroes bring out their entire library – *The Farmer's Almanac, The Bouncy Twins at Camp Wahoo,* and even Bullwinkle's personal volume of *Ghastly Comix* – to help the moon men pass the citizenship test. Unfortunately, Rocky and Bullwinkle's ideas of what the moon men need to learn turn out to be along the lines of how many days in September (eighty!) and how do you make fire without matches (Rub two Scouts – that is, two *sticks* – together!). In fact, so badly do Gidney and Cloyd do on the test that the senator orders them deported…back to the moon! All official Washington turns out to watch the departure, but when Bullwinkle accidentally catches Senator Fussmussen's jacket when he slams closed the spaceship hatch, the President has no choice but to appoint the senator the first interplanetary ambassador!

BOX TOP ROBBERY

EPISODES 41–52

YOU SAY YOU SUSPECT SOMETHING SNEAKY'S GOING ON

with the world economy? You are not alone. The second story arc, "Box Top Robbery," begins with the revelation that box tops are the *real* basis of the world's monetary system, and, moreover – horrors! – they're being counterfeited. Suspicion falls instantly on the owner of the planet's largest collection of *genuine* box tops, none other than Bullwinkle J. Moose. (Incidentally, all this attention on counterfeit cereal box tops, weird contests, and the like didn't exactly endear Ward Productions to the sponsor – a cereal company.)

Forty-one

An emergency session of the World Economic Council is horrified to learn someone is counterfeiting box tops, the true basis of the world economy, and suspicion falls immediately on Bullwinkle J. Moose of Frostbite Falls, Minnesota, owner of the world's largest collection of genuine

box tops. When Mister Moose and Rocket J. Squirrel attempt to open a box-top account at the Swineherds' and Farmers' National Bank, the police collar the moose, clapping him into the patrol wagon and whisking him away.

Forty-two

Round one of the battle of the box tops goes to Boris Badenov, who has succeeded in dumping thousands of counterfeits on the market, cleaning out the premiums in store after store. As a result, box-top savers across the country see their savings wiped out. Things are tough all over, especially behind police headquarters, where Bullwinkle is still being questioned.

Forty-three

Rocky tells the council that one of its own is in cahoots with the box-top bad man. Why? Because the phony box tops are even showing up

in Whatchacallistan, which is so remote that only members of the World Economic Council know where it is.

Forty-four

When Boris Badenov locks our heroes in a clock tower, the mighty moose hurls himself at the locked door, but bounces right into the whirling mass of machinery instead.

Forty-five

Rocky searches for something to smash open the tower door and help his pal. The hammer he hurls barely misses Bullwinkle's head, but the vibration that follows knocks the agile moose out the window and onto a precarious Harold Lloydish perch on the clock face.

Forty-six

Bullwinkle is pavement-bound, for Boris Badenov, disguised as the pipe-puffing Detective Hemlock Soames, has thrown him a rope, but failed to fasten the other end. Just as doom appears near, Rocky the flying squirrel swoops to his friend's defense, grabbing the loose rope and fastening it to a flagpole, which bends like a fishing rod when the moose reaches the end of his tether, snapping the moose right back up through a window and into the conference room of the World Economic Council, where a meeting is in progress.

Forty-seven

Searching for the box-top bad man, the perspicacious moose walks right into an abandoned elevator shaft and discovers the counterfeit box-top hideout below. Meanwhile, at the building's back entrance, Boris and Natasha are busily shoveling their booty into a huge truck.

Forty-eight

Innocently stepping inside a down elevator, Rocky and Bullwinkle are shot high into the sky when a bomb planted by Boris explodes! As they hurtle toward earth, the chairman of the World Economic Council picks up the trail of the box-top bad man.

Forty-nine

Another fiendish scheme foiled: When Boris and Natasha try to drive a truck full of counterfeit box tops across the state line, they're stopped by an open drawbridge. But just as the police arrive, the dastardly duo decamps, leaping over the side of the bridge.

Fifty

Having splashed down in an elevator car, our heroes are now afloat on the open sea. When a coast guard cutter approaches, rescue seems near…until the ship's captain, taking them for enemy agents, fires depth charges in their direction.

Fifty-one

Rocky and Bullwinkle may be free again, but it seems you can't keep a bad man down, for after all his troubles and fouled-up plans, Boris Badenov is back in business again…turning out four million counterfeit box tops, enough to wreck the entire American economy!

Fifty-two

Unaware that the box-top bad man's secret printing press is nearby, Rocky and Bullwinkle decide to have a reward poster printed up. While they sit on a park bench designing it, a surreptitiously placed stick of dynamite sizzles next to them. But when Bullwinkle blithely returns the dynamite to Boris, the secret headquarters is blown up, the American economy is saved, and Rocky and Bullwinkle ride off into the sunset after getting official hero medals.

And now here to tell you everything about anything is...

MR. KNOW-IT-ALL

Hello, Knowledge Thirsters. Today's subject is "How to Sell Vacuum Cleaners...and Clean Up." The two prime requisites in selling vacuum cleaners are the custom-oar and the custom-ee. The custom-oar, or victim, usually lives in a house. The custom-ee, or salesman, has to get into the house.

Rule Number One: Always get your foot in the custom-oar's door. Good morning, custom-oar, would you be –

(BONK!!)

Rule Number Two: Forget about Rule Number One! Also at this point forget about getting in the door and find another way of getting in...such as a window!

(KEE-RASH!!!!)

Preferably an open window. If the custom-oar complains about the mess – Oh, pshaw, I shall rectify *that* in a jiffy!

(KAFF-KAFF!!!!)

Just make certain when cleaning up, you don't suck up the entire room *and* the custom-ee – that is, yourself – into the vacuum as well!

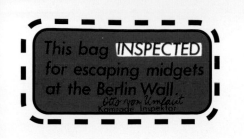

Cut out & Paste on luggage, Briefcase or lunch bucket

OUR STORY OPENS IN THE POST OFFICE

of Frostbite Falls, Minnesota, where Bullwinkle J. Moose has received a letter informing him that he's inherited a mine from his late uncle Dewlap. No one knows just what kind of mine it might be, but someone certainly wants to keep our heroes away from it.

Fifty-four

With more courage than brains, our heroes set off for the mysterious Mount Flatten, site of Uncle Dewlap's mine, blithely marching into a mine field on a secret military reservation after a mysterious motorcyclist (by the name of Boris Badenov) has switched the roadside signs. Are they on the Road to Ruin?

Fifty-five

Trapped in the middle of a mine field on a secret desert missile base might be trouble enough for some people, but not for Bullwinkle, who's ready to say "Yer welcome" when Rocky spots tanks.

Fifty-six

Stranded in the desert, at first our boys are glad to see the mysterious long black car that stops to pick them up, but then they notice there are no door handles or window cranks (much less power windows). The driver turns out to be a real dummy too, as the limo hurtles down the road.

Fifty-seven

Still trying to get to Bullwinkle's inheritance, Rocky and Bullwinkle have been misdirected by Boris and Natasha, and now a mysterious stranger is remotely controlling their driverless limousine as it races across the desert. When the mysterious stranger guiding the speeding auto presses the wrong button, the limo…EXPLODES!

Fifty-eight

Wandering in the desert after your remotely controlled limousine is torn apart because someone who sounds remarkably like Captain "Wrong Way" Peachfuzz pressed the wrong button can really leave a moose parched, and craving a

nice ice cream sodey. But it's just a mirage, Rocky reasurres his pal. "You know what a mirage is, doncha?" Of course Bullwinkle does, it's where you park your car. Meanwhile, Boris and Natasha are fiendishly planning on a nearby hill.

Fifty-nine

It's mighty dry in the desert, where the mighty moose would give anything for a drop of water, even the deed to Uncle

Dewlap's mine. No sooner said than Gunga Drain, a professional Indian-type water boy, shows up to peddle his watery wares. When Rocky turns him down, the wily water boy with the Pottsylvanian accent offers our heroes souvenir pin-on badges, which actually are deadly poisonous scorpions.

Sixty

Deeper into the desert they stagger, while high above our heroes a mysterious helicopter circles. When the copter comes bonging down on Bullwinkle, his antlers tangle in the landing gear and up he goes with the erratically ascending whirlybird!

Sixty-one

Bullwinkle's hanging from the ping-ponging gyrocopter and Rocky's hanging from Bullwinkle, until the confused mysterious stranger pulls a wrong lever and they tumble inside the copter cabin to be reunited with Captain Peter "Wrong Way" Peachfuzz. Mysterious no longer, but just as confused as ever, he pulls yet another wrong lever, blowing the blades off the battered flying machine. Peachfuzz and Bullwinkle parachute out of the disabled craft, while Rocky soars to earth.

Sixty-two

Hopelessly turned around after their dizzying helicopter flight, the boys still have to find Mount Flatten, which, says Captain Peachfuzz, the head of the secret G-2 intelligence agency, contains "upsidasium," vital to the national defense.

Sixty-three

Boris briefly entertains a Fiendish Plan for supplanting Peachfuzz as head of American intelligence, but gives up on the idea when he realizes that the riches he would gain selling state secrets would bring him to the attention of the infernal Internal Revenue Service. Instead, Abou Ben Boris soon appears and tricks our heroes, sending Bullwinkle to dreamland, then – drawing a wicked sword – sneaking up behind Rocky and Peachfuzz.

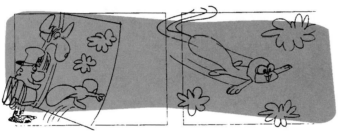

Sixty-four

After eluding Boris again, our heroes are off into the trackless desert. But it turns out there *are* tracks in the trackless desert after all, and Captain Peachfuzz has found them: railroad tracks to be exact!

Sixty-five

On board a speeding train, on the perilous path to Mount Flatten and Bullwinkle's inherited upsidasium mine, our heroes listen as Captain Peachfuzz explains what the rare and valuable metal actually is.

Sixty-six

The story of the discovery of the fabulous antigravity metal, as told by Captain Peter Peachfuzz, continues: Some years back, in the little desert town of Buzzards Craw, a grizzled

prospector had appeared holding a rope at the end of which, like some braying kite, floated his trusted burro. Mere days later, at the Durango Assay Office, upsidasium was rather precipitously unveiled to an incredulous world. As soon as the box containing the antigravity metal was opened, the world's entire supply of upsidasium shot into the sky, and when the grizzled old prospector tried to file a claim on the elusive flying Mount Flatten, he discovered it was already owned by one Dewlap D. Moose.

Sixty-seven

At a desert train stop, Rocky and Bullwinkle run into two familiar faces with unfamiliar names. Yes, it's Mojave Max, GOP – which stands, of course, for grizzled old prospector – and his partner, Death Valley Dotty, who greets our heroes with a hearty, "Howdy partner, dollink." While Bullwinkle is busily heeding Rocky's admonition not to reveal anything about the top-secret lost mountain, their train departs without them.

Sixty-eight

Slowly, our heroes are closing in on the lost mountain and Bullwinkle's upsidasium mine. Then they find some primitive markers pointing the way to Mount Flatten, but the last marker points right back to the way they've come. Realizing they couldn't've passed it, Rocky and Bullwinkle gaze up: There, hovering miles above their heads, is an enormous regulation-size mountain peak.

Sixty-nine

An abandoned mine shaft fiendishly disguised to look like an elevator sends Bullwinkle plummeting, with Rocky plunging after to save him. Too late, Boris realizes that without Moose he cannot find floating Flatten Peak.

"I hate those no-goodniks, Moose and Squirrel!"

Seventy

Well, they've finally made it! Accompanied by those two GOPs, Mojave Max and Death Valley Dotty, Rocky and Bullwinkle reach the floating mountain. When Boris goes to clobber the unsuspecting Rocky with a huge boulder, the upsidasium-filled rock zips instead right into the sky.

Seventy-one

Finally on Mount Flatten itself, our heroes begin the search for Bullwinkle's inherited mine. The method they choose to communicate with Captain Peachfuzz turns out to be not exactly top secret. Rocky and Bullwinkle send out smoke signals and soon everyone in the country knows about the fabulous Mount Flatten. Tourists begin to descend.

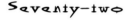

Seventy-two

In the search for the upsidasium mine, Bullwinkle unearths a large antigrav-metal-filled boulder and promptly finds himself falling up into the sky. But as he chips pieces away, back down he comes. Meanwhile, Boris and Natasha are proceeding with their Fiendish Plan – as detailed in Uncle Vanya's *Fireside Crook Book* – to steal Mount Flatten right out from under the U.S. government's nose.

Seventy-three

Rocky and Bullwinkle may have discovered a rich lode of upsidasium on Mount Flatten, but, because it's the only known substance in the universe that falls upward, there's the small difficulty of

figuring out how to hold on to it. Meanwhile, as Boris and Natasha are proceeding with their plan to abscond with the floating mountain, they get a call from Central Control: Mister Big is flying toward them in an ominous black jet!

Seventy-four

Our heroes are having such a hard time holding on to any sky-climbing upsidasium that they need to consult an expert, so they set off in search of

Mojave Max, actually their worst enemy, Boris Badenov, who's busily perusing his *Fireside Crook Book,* searching for just the right Fiendish Plan to steal the entire mountain. When Moose and Squirrel show up, they considerately offer to lead

him and Natasha directly back to their mine. So, as our two heroes lower themselves into the mine at his suggestion, Boris gives them the shaft, hurling a huge boulder down at them. Up above, Boris is feeling so good about his badness that he's even contemplating double-crossing the dread Mister Big, a figure who casts an ominous shadow. Meanwhile, just seconds away from complete disaster, it's Bullwinkle at the Bottom, or, Mishmash Moose!

Seventy-five

Back in Washington, the files on upsidasium are so secret, even Captain Peachfuzz's secretary can't look for them with her eyes open, so the good captain does the obvious: He turns on the Rocky show for an update, then takes a fast jet straight to the North Pole! Meanwhile, back at Mount Flatten, our heroes narrowly dodge the descending boulder and begin the long rope climb back up the mine shaft, while Boris and Natasha try to placate the implacable Mister Big, whose voice is a sinister Peter Lorre-ish whisper. But the danger above is matched by the danger below, when Rocky spies a rapidly approaching jet! It's Double Trouble, or, The Moose Hangs High!

Seventy-six

Boris impresses Mister Big by just nicking the rope from which our heroes are dangling, making it fray a bit at a time, so that their danger is prolonged! Below, Bullwinkle just can't imagine who's flying that mysterious jet upside down directly underneath. Could it be Captain Peachfuzz, a close friend who's getting just a little too close for comfort? Rocky zooms into the air and immediately spots the problem: Captain Peachfuzz is sitting the wrong way in his pilot's seat! Just as the rope breaks and Bullwinkle plunges toward the ground, the fearless squirrel flies into the cockpit and takes over at the controls, maneuvering the out-of-control jet so that the falling moose can snag the tail – of the plane, that is! But still the jet falls toward earth! Will Jet Jockey Rocky make a One-Point Landing?

Seventy-seven

Everything's fine and dandy for our jet-plane-flying heroes…if you look at the picture *sideways,* that is; otherwise, they're hurtling at supersonic speed straight toward the ground! As soon as quick-thinking Rocky hears that the jet was designed by none other than "Wrong Way" Peachfuzz himself, he knows just what to do: He works the controls backward! So, for Boris and Natasha, it's back to the ol' *Crook Book* for more nefarious recipes, and for our heroes it's down to a safe landing, coincidentally right next to Mister Big's hideout, where Rocky comes up with a bright idea, but Bullwinkle's dubious and has only two words to say: Im-possible!

Seventy-eight

Shhh! Rocky and Bullwinkle have a secret plan of their own: Fasten Captain Peachfuzz's jet engine to the mountain and secretly fly it to Washington, D.C.! But on the far side of Mount Flatten, Boris and Natasha have a plan too. Unfortunately, after hours of

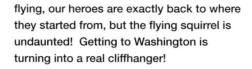

flying, our heroes are exactly back to where they started from, but the flying squirrel is undaunted! Getting to Washington is turning into a real cliffhanger!

Seventy-nine

The upsidasium-filled mountain is acting more like a granite yo-yo, and now our heroes know the reason why: On the far side of the mountain is a second, opposing jet engine, and operating it are Mojave Max and Death Valley Dotty, who, when discovered, immediately flee! Meanwhile, the capital is abuzz with anticipation and excitement as the flying mountain finally approaches. But Boris vows to put the motto of Terrorist Tech into effect: WHEN IN DOUBT, BLOW IT UP!

Eighty

Mister Big fills Boris in on why Pottsylvania must have that upsidasium, or make certain that no one else has it either: It seems that some years ago, Pottsylvanian assembly lines started turning out thousands of Assassin Eight automobiles, which, in a country with only six miles of road, now all sit gridlocked. Yes, if all the Assassin Eights in Pottsylvania were laid end to end, it would be a typical Sunday afternoon, so only the antigravity metal will cure the huge parking problem! Now Boris sees his duty clearly: It's the Big Blast, or, a Many-Splintered Thing!

Eighty-one

Mister Big orders Boris to blow himself up with the mountain as punishment for failing to steal the upsidasium, but the Big Guy concludes he's been hasty when Boris reminds him that *he'll* be blown to hasty pudding too, so Mister Big prudently takes a powder while Rocky and Bullwinkle are greeted by Washington senators (out of uniform too, Bullwinkle notices) as they bring the upsidasium-filled mountain safely to Fort Knick Knack, where its upsidasium is carefully mined. Soon Boris, under fiendish instructions from Mister Big, sneaks into our heroes' room and – while they innocently snooze– steals Rocky's goggles and flying helmet! Shortly thereafter, a Pottsylvanian-accented flying squirrel with a moustache hokey-smokes his nefarious way right past the fort's guards and into the upsidasium-filled vault! It looks like the biggest robbery in history…that's right, The Steal Hour, or…A Snitch in Time!

Eighty-two

Back at the Up at Arms, a Washington hotel, our heroes awaken and realize that the missing goggles mean fiendishness is afoot, so they hasten – still in their nightclothes – to Forth Knick Knack, where the dastardly spies are using powerful magnets to load the nation's entire strategic reserve of upsidasium into a waiting fleet of trucks! Will General Broadbeam and our boys get there in time, or will Mister Big just keep getting bigger?

Eighty-three

IF IT'S WORTH STEALING AT ALL, STEAL IT ALL, declaims Boris as he and Natasha go out the window just before our heroes and General Broadbeam rush in. But where are their trucks, and more to the point, thinks General Broadbeam, where'd those flying goggles that the moose has picked up near the window come from? Naturally, using his rapier-like military intelligence, the general reaches an instant conclusion and has Rocky arrested, but when the squirrel reminds the general that they've been together all along, General Broadbeam once again draws the obvious conclusion…and has himself arrested! But where's the upsidasium? wonders Bullwinkle. Could it've just disappeared into thin air? That's precisely where the fleet of trucks is, floating upward! Are these Truck Drivers in the Sky, and can our heroes Follow the Fleet?

Eighty-four

To corral the rapidly departing fleet of flying trucks, Rocky rockets over to the nearby missile base, but the military's rule is NO SQUIRRELS ON MISSILES, so our quick-thinking hero has General Broadbeam name him nosecone first class, and soon he's blasted into space. But the missile's being tracked by powerful radar in another country, and the Rocky-ridden rocket reverses course! Target: the White House, Washington, D.C.

Eighty-five

It's two seconds to DESTRUCT when Rocket J. manages to fix the errant missile's controls and send it back after the flying trucks. Soon he's rounding up the fleet, but when his lead vehicle runs out of gas, they all start drifting back up again, until mighty Bullwinkle ties a heavy rope to a rock and flings it over the fleeing fleet.

Eighty-six

Rocky and Bullwinkle race off in pursuit of the fleeing Badenov, but his general disguise has more stars than the real general has, so it's Broadbeam who gets hauled off to the brig. Meanwhile, back in a storage room, our heroes have stumbled upon the shadowy Mister Big's

hiding place. But when they go to rush him…it's The Battle of the Giants, or, It Takes Two to Tangle!

Eighty-seven

Well, Mister Big has turned out to be quite tiny after all, but Rocky and Bullwinkle's troubles look huge! While in a guardhouse outside General Broadbeam takes an examination to determine if he will be sentenced to the jute mill or the rock pile for his crime, and the little Big Guy is left all alone in a vault filled with upsidasium as our heroes get taken to a sinister-looking wall by a general who looks an awful lot like Boris Badenov.

Eighty-eight

Boris orders the firing squad to fire, but he inadvertently has them facing in the wrong direction. While he's trying to get them the right way again, the general's timely arrival saves our heroes. Rocky goes after Mister Big, who's trying to get away with his ill-gotten antigravity gains, but Mister B. captures Rocket J. and it looks as if he just might get away. But the greedy criminal mastermind won't let go of the floating metal and he's lifted upward, disappearing forever into the sky.

METAL-MUNCHING MICE

EPISODES 89–104

IN THE PRESENT COMFORTABLY HIGH-TECH ERA

with cable TV, home video, fiber optics, geosynchronous satellites, PCs, and the mighty zapper – it might be easy to forget what a threat to Western civilization giant metal-munching mice who loved to feast on TV antennae might have once seemed.

Eighty-nine

Our story opens in the quaint hamlet of Frostbite Falls, Minnesota, the only town in the United States with more TV sets than people. The reason for this astounding fact is simple: This is the home of one of television's most sparkling personalities…none other than Rocket J. Squirrel. But, mysteriously, every TV antenna in town has disappeared, making reception of the over-the-air TV signal impossible!

Ninety

The calm reaction of the Frostbite Falls citizenry ("Our lives are ruined!") to the lack of television spurs our heroes to action. Assigned to stand guard over a decoy antenna, Bullwinkle J. Moose comes face-to-face with what appears to be a six-foot-tall metal mouse. The meeting lasts only a few exciting seconds and then Bullwinkle sleeps soundly until morning. Of course, when he awakens, he finds it impossible to tell anyone about the close encounter.

Ninety-one

Perhaps the mystery of the nation's disappearing TV antennae will be solved after all: Rocket J. Squirrel has just been appointed to head the investigation by glad-handing Senator Shunpike.

Ninety-two

There's trouble for our heroes in creepy old Bleakly House, where Rocky and Bullwinkle have set a giant mousetrap: Bullwinkle triggers the trap, firing himself almost all the way through a window high above the ground, while Rocky, wandering dazed in the gloom, confronts an astounding six-foot-tall sight!

Ninety-three

On the track of the gigantic mouse again, our heroes charge down a secret Bleakly House passageway. Coming upon a closed door, Bullwinkle puts his ear to it to listen in and promptly gets his head stuck. Suddenly, the door is yanked open and Bullwinkle flies into the room, where Rocky sees an awful apparition.

Ninety-four

The leader of the metal-munching mechanical moon mice, the Mickey Mouse-eared Big Cheese himself (who has a vaguely familiar face and a pronounced Pottsylvanian accent), outlines his plan for bringing civilization to its knees: First eliminate the TV antennae, then the television transmitters, then the country is finished, deserted by its own citizenry. And number one on the no-goodnik's Kaput Parade…the Rocky and Bullwinkle show!

Ninety-five

The Big Cheese's scorched air policy is working: Americans are deserting their TV-less country in droves! But not really: The pictures are actually of Pottsylvania! Pursued by Herman the Mechanical Vermin Exterminator, our heroes stop short, but the mechanical mouse stops even shorter, having wound down.

Ninety-six

There's no choice but to return to Bleakly House mansion, dread home of the mechanical mice! Once they're inside, Boris dispatches an entire

platoon of mechanical metal-munching mice after our heroes, who have to come up fast with an answer, but not necessarily the one Bullwinkle has: Vienna, Austria, in 1758! When the mice attack, Rocky acts fast, gumming up the works by feeding the mysterious metal munchers chewy caramel, which temporarily keeps them from opening their mouths to bite anything!

Ninety-seven

The Big Cheese doesn't curdle at all when a flying saucer descends from the heavens, disgorging more six-foot-tall mechanical mice. Will the Fiendish Plan succeed after all? Bullwinkle's not sure, because it's tough to follow the plot and be in it at the same time! It's a first-class Fiendish Plan, though – Natasha says proudly – having been disapproved by *Bad Housekeeping* magazine. Meanwhile, our heroes sneak up on the mysterious spaceship.

Ninety-eight

A strange space weapon has been fired, and it's Big Cheese Boris who's scrooched straighter than a boiled shirt! Cloyd and Gidney, the two moon men, are back. Meanwhile, as soon as he's unscrooched, the cheese unleashes a veritable army of mechanical mice at Podunk Junction, his carefully chosen target (using his throw-dart-at-map strategy), but our heroes head 'em off – where else? – at the pass!

Ninety-nine

The thundering herd approaches, but, by taking the expressway instead of the pass, the metal munchers descend on Podunk Junction unopposed. Program after program goes off the air, and in a remarkably short time, television is off all over town! Desperate to stop the monstrous mechanical metal-munching moon mice, Rocky and Bullwinkle take out a newspaper advertisement – MAKE BIG MONEY! WHISTLE WHILE YOU WORK! – seeking one genuine pied piper. They get results quicker than expected when their ad is answered instantly by one Mister Chasemoff, a piper with a peck full of impeccable credentials, a vaguely familiar face, and a thick foreign (could it be Pottsylvanian?) accent. At a buck a moon mouse, it'll be Bucks for Boris if Rocky Pays the Piper!

One hundred

Line after line of moon mice seem to be leaving town, but at the end of the day there seem to be more than ever! However did one hundred thousand monstrous metal-munching moon mice come to be on earth anyway? It seems that the Man in the Moon is now Mister Big, who'd gotten all the way to the moon after last we saw him greedily clutching upsidasium and floating up into space! And what's more, he's taken over too! It looks A Fright Flight on a Rocky to the Moon!

One hundred & one

Bullwinkle thinks a little cheery music would do everyone a world of good, so he decides to give a ukulele concert, which is interrupted by the appearance of thousands of monstrous mechanical moon mice.

One hundred & two

Bullwinkle's singing may have attracted all the mechanical moon mice, but, not to be outdone, the Big Cheese grabs a balalaika and croons a few tunes of his own.

One hundred & three

Bullwinkle's new manager, Colonel Tomsk Parkoff, has a pronounced Pottsylvanian accent and big plans for the moose's singing career: The warbling, ukulele-playing moose will be playing to an SRO crowd of metal-munching moon mice that's packed Colossus Stadium.

One hundred & four

Boris is up to his explosive old tricks, planning to blow up one and all in the packed stadium, while the pompadoured and neon-jacketed rock-god moose strums an electrified ukulele and croons for his metal-munching fans. But the fiendish plan blows up in Boris's face when the explosion hurtles the mouse-filled stadium all the way back to the moon, destroying Mister Big's spaceship in the process. Our heroes have come through once again!

BABY FACE
BRAUNSCHWEIGER

GOOGLE
BOID

"I was cuke as a coolcumber..."

GREENPERNT OOGLE

IF IT'S CLOTHES THAT MAKE THE MAN

then it sometimes seems that it's footwear, or at least feet, that make the moose. Take, for example, this brief saga of the weathercasting bunion and the wondrous fortune-telling bird.

One hundred & five

Bullwinkle's very own, celebrated, prophesyin', weather-forecastin' bunion has him and Rocky in deep trouble: Two mysterious figures have entered the little Frostbite Falls house where our heroes reside, tied and gagged Rocky, and put Bullwinkle in dreamland with a knockout sleeping potion. Carefully, they pack up the snoozing moose's

prescient tootsies and hustle them and their owner out into the night.

One hundred & six

A plane carrying Bullwinkle to who-knows-what-fate heads out over the ocean while the stout-hearted squirrel trudges from government office to government office, trying to get help for his pal. At the Weather Bureau, Rocky gets his first glimpse of modern, scientific weather forecasting.

One hundred & seven

Finally, someone to listen to his story: none other than the head of the scientifically state-of-the-art Weather Bureau, Captain Peter "Wrong Way" Peachfuzz himself! Attempting to contact the White House, Peachfuzz punches the wrong button on his high-tech desk, making inadvertent connection with the Air Defense Command.

One hundred & eight

Bullwinkle and his much-in-demand digits may be miles out to sea aboard a mystery plane, but Rocky and Peachfuzz are

OOGLE BOID

now in hotfooted pursuit. As they draw near, a menacing-looking weapon points out of the back of the mystery plane at them.

One hundred & nine

While Rocky and Captain Peachfuzz drift on a raft in the ocean, Bullwinkle wakes to find himself in a magnificently appointed apartment, his foot with the weather-forecasting bunion perched delicately on a velvet cushion. Soon he's talking to Bushwick the Thirty-third, the little king of the tiny island of Greenpernt, who's brought along a huge headsman with a sharp ax.

One hundred & ten

The king tells Bullwinkle the tale of the fabulous Greenpernt oogle bird, which lays only one egg a month, but it's a doozie: Each egg contains a fortune that foretells the future!

One hundred & eleven

Rocky and Peachfuzz, desperately paddling against the tide, are trying to reach the tiny island of Greenpernt. Meanwhile, the king orders Bullwinkle to act as substitute wizard in place of the stolen oogle bird, whose predictions had been the source of all of Greenpernt's now-departed good fortune.

One hundred & twelve

Rocky and Bullwinkle are reunited thanks to Captain Peachfuzz's wrong-way plan, but soon all three are at the mercy of King Bushwick the Thirty-third.

One hundred & thirteen

From tracks on the beach, Rocky deduces that the oogle has been birdnapped. Even now the fortune-telling bird is held captive in Boris Badenov's heavily defended island fortress.

One hundred & fourteen

Mounting an expeditionary force to recapture the fabulous fowl, the captain, the king, and our two heroes are about to hit the beach, where Boris is preparing an explosive welcome.

One hundred & fifteen

In the hunt for the Greenpernt oogle, Rocky and Bullwinkle have so far succeeded only in capturing each other. Then they spy a huge boulder rolling down the hill at them…only it isn't a boulder at all,

it's a fortune-telling oogle bird egg, which cracks open and prophesies that "when you get this fortune egg, you climb the hill and shake a leg."

One hundred & sixteen

On the top of the hill, our heroes find the purloined predictor. Boris has a Fiendish Plan to stop them, but he's trapped instead in his own mine fields. When everyone returns to Greenpernt, Peter Peachfuzz replaces the reluctant oogle as the island's resident wizard, and by doing the exact opposite of what "Wrong Way" Peachfuzz advises, the tiny island prospers as never before.

RUE BRITTANIA

EPISODES 117–124

IT'S THE BULLWINKLE PEDAL EXTREMITY

that once again kicks off this adventure. Will the debonair moose finally take his place as a member of the peerage and come into his true noble inheritance?

One hundred & seventeen

When the noble but forgetful Earl of Crankcase takes a high dive into an empty pool, the nephews (Filcher, Belcher, and, ahem, Jay) gather at the prestigious law firm of Lamb, Curry & Rice for the reading of the will. A million-pound note goes to the new earl, identified only by a photograph of a foot on which is inscribed *Rue Brittania*. Naturally enough, the foot turns out to belong to a moose, and the moose in

EARL AND WATER DON'T MIX

NEXT TIME TAKE THE DRAIN

question turns out to reside in Frostbite Falls, Minnesota. When Rocky and Bullwinkle set sail for the ancestral homeland of the Crankcases, the three nefarious nephews set out to do them in.

One hundred & eighteen

The S.S. *Flotsam*, the luxurious ocean liner carrying our heroes to England, is sunk, but Rocky and Bullwinkle make it to shore. There they get

into a peculiar taxicab with three suspicious-appearing drivers who drive them directly to the White Cliffs of Dover, where they're foiled in their attempt to do Rocky and Bullwinkle in. Upon hoofing it back to London, our heroes learn that the million-pound inheritance will be Bullwinkle's just as soon as he's spent a week in the ancestral manse, Abominable Manor.

MOOSE GETS THE JUICE

ELECTRICITY DANGER

MOURNING BECOMES ELECTRA-CUTED

One hundred & nineteen

Rocky and Bullwinkle aren't particularly fond of the gloomy furnishings at Abominable Manor… particularly the Burmese tiger trap.

One hundred & twenty

In an explosive situation, the call goes out for the exterminator, whose job is not to make it worse, it's Badenov.

ABOMINABLE MANOR

MR. KNOW-IT-ALL

Today's subject is "How to Get into the Movies...Without Buying a Ticket." The first approach is to go directly to the manager and say, "Where's my pass?"

(KEE-RASH!!!!)

Unruffled by that minor setback, we try Phase Two, which involves a disguise: "Hello there, I'm Flo Ziegfeld, how's my show going tonight?"

(KEE-RASH!!!!)

Phase Three: Seeking out the location of the freight elevator, we then proceed down into the basement, where we shall then proceed up to the balcony.

(KEE-RASH!!!!)

Hmm, that's the deepest basement I ever saw. On to Phase Four: "Hello, Mr. Theater Manager, I should like to apply for a job as an usher. After all,

I been in the dark most of my life." And sure enough, it's a deal: The job is ours and it pays a princely sum: a box of popcorn and all the ticket stubs we can collect. So donning our usherette's uniform, we take up our post in the mezzanine. Only make sure you don't accidentally stroll into the projection room, or soon you'll find yourself ushering at a theater that's closed for repairs!

"Sure is dark in here."

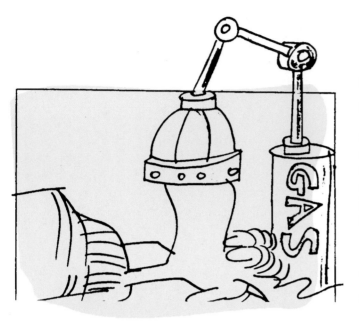

One hundred & twenty-two

A faulty fuse box in Abominable Manor saves Bullwinkle some unnecessary cuts, but he may be cut out of his inheritance anyway.

One hundred & twenty-three

Boris Badenov, that Dracula of the cartoon industry, lures our heroes into a conveniently constructed rocket ship.

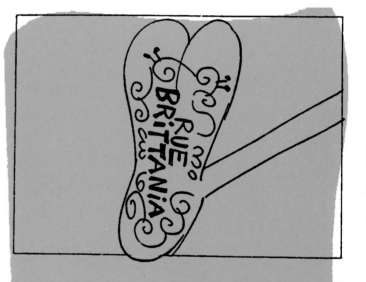

One hundred & twenty-four

Boris slips Moose and Squirrel knockout drops, but they come to just in time for the end of the story: The inscription turns out to have been caused by a bathmat, and it's faded from Bullwinkle's foot, so the nefarious nephews are saddled with the inherited million-pound *promissory* note after all, while Boris and Natasha are last seen orbiting in their runaway spaceship, somewhere in the outer reaches of the Milky Way. Funny how that bathmat inscription fooled everyone, says Rocky. Yeah, agrees the amiable moose, but what's *really* funny is the *Rue Brittania* inscription on my *other* foot, which *never* comes off.

One hundred & twenty-one

Boris vows a "change of earl," so he disguises himself first as a British bobby and then as a surgeon all too eager to operate on the belly-aching Bullwinkle, who's pigged out on Macadamia nuts.

MR. KNOW-iT-ALL

I was wondering why they always call me fathead. Our subject is from my bestselling book, *How to Win Friends and Be Influential with People.* I quote: "Pick out something about a person that you admire. Tell them about it, and they surely will be your friend." But…make certain the person's hair you have chosen to admire is not detachable! "Learn the interests and hobbies of those you would like to have as your friend." At the Villains Athletic Club, for example, I have studied all of the subjects that interest a certain kindly Pottsylvanian sportsman, who favors bowling, baseball, and croquet. There he is now. Hello there, kindly –

(KEE-RA5H!!!!)

From my bestselling book, page thirty-five, I quote: "Sometimes those you seek may seem standoffish. Obviously, they are just shy."

Obviously the case here. It simply means you must bring them out by doing little favors, like carrying this here ticking box out of this top-secret government vault –

(KEE-RA5H!!!!)

Oh well, there *is* one man who's promised to be my friend for life: The publisher… if I never write another book!

BURIED TREASURE

EPISODES 125–138

CIRCULATION IS WAY DOWN

at the *Frostbite Falls Picayune Intelligence* newspaper, so its owner, Colonel McCornpone, tries to boost sales by sponsoring a buried-treasure hunt. The prize: one million dollars buried in the Picayune Pot and a genuine 1910 Stearn-Knight Runabout, a snazzy classic auto. The catch: It's Confederate money, son.

One hundred & twenty-six

With the Frostbite Falls citizenry in the grip of the buried-treasure craze, all the likely spots in town have already been dug up, so Bullwinkle sets off to dig in *un*likely spots – like outside a refinery, where the moose promptly strikes oil, a feat that lands him in the town calaboose. Taking advantage of the treasure hunt, Babyface Boris Braunschweiger, the "Minnesota Monster," a Pottsylvanian-accented master criminal, and his gang, the Lightfingered Five Minus Two, show up to dig...straight into the bank.

BABY FACE BRAUNSCHWEIGER

One hundred & twenty-seven

Rocky's lonesome for Bullwinkle, who, to get his mind off the buried treasure, has set off on his bicycle to visit relatives in Ponca City. So Rocky goes after his friend,

DYNAMITE

but runs into Babyface and his gang digging outside town. Before you can say "Hokey smoke!" the plucky squirrel's bound and blindfolded next to a big stick of dynamite with a short fuse.

One hundred & twenty-eight

In the bank basement, the Lightfingered Five Minus Two are cleaning up. Meanwhile, Bullwinkle is speeding up...as he bicycles backward down a steep hill.

One hundred & twenty-nine

Rocky may very well be all up in the air over the dastardly bank stickup, but he's about to come down...hard. It looks like a clean getaway for Babyface Boris and his new bunch of baddie buddies.

One hundred & thirty

Rocky's survived his fall with nothing more than a bonk to the noggin, while Babyface Boris and his gang are making their getaway in the fastest car in Frostbite Falls (also the only), a stolen 1910 Stearns-Knight Runabout, with Bullwinkle on his bicycle in determined pursuit – until an elderly chipmunk in the middle of the road causes him to come to a screeching halt.

DOWN TO EARTH

ME AND MY SHATTER

another suitor, a smitten Bullwinkle J. Moose, but it's the suitor's suitcase that's most suitable for swiping, so Boris promptly absconds.

One hundred & thirty-one

The crash leaves Bullwinkle with amnesia and Boris with Bullwinkle's valise, which contains socks and a peanut butter sandwich. The still-addled moose is puzzled because the money in *his* straw valise doesn't look like *real* Confederate dollars, but suspiciously like greenbacks instead.

One hundred & thirty-two

A fortuitous lightning strike takes out the Lightfingered Five Minus Two, who had been getting testy about their share of the loot anyway. While searching for Bullwinkle, Rocky uses his trusty Mother Moose Call, but instead winds up fetching the fetching Honeychile Moosemoss, just in from the Ever-glades, a cutie with a more than passing resemblance to a certain Pottsylvanian bad guy.

One hundred & thirty-three

Honeychile Moosemoss, a Badenov gal from way below the Mooson-Dixon line, captures yet

One hundred & thirty-four

It looks like a triple cross to the Lightfingered Five Minus Two: Boris buys a ticket to Skinnyapolis, but makes his getaway on a railroad handcar that bangs right into Bullwinkle.

One hundred & thirty-five

Our quick-witted heroes have switched suitcases yet again and made off on the railroad handcar with Boris and the Lightfingered Five Minus Two in

hot pursuit in the 1910 Sterns-Knight Runabout. Once back in Frostbite Falls, it's after banking hours, and they won't take back the stolen money, so Bullwinkle has to get himself arrested to protect the suitcase full of loot.

One hundred & thirty-six

Snatching back the suitcase full of stolen loot calls for a master plan, but Boris and gang can't even seem to get arrested, so they go the underground route instead, and soon they've tunneled right in on Bullwinkle.

One hundred & thirty-seven

The Lightfingered Five Minus Two puts Bullwinkle temporarily on ice. Meanwhile, Boris may finally have the right suitcase, but all the money's blowing in the breeze, so Rocky hooks himself up to a super vacuum cleaner and flies through town, cleaning up.

One hundred & thirty-eight

In sweeping up the stolen bank loot, Rocky picks up a particularly large crumb, none other than Babyface Boris himself, who takes off in hot pursuit. Rocky has a cool idea for refuge: The icehouse where the trapped Bullwinkle has frozen almost solid (well, his stare is icy anyway). Trying to hide the stolen money, they instead find the Picayune Pot, winning the vintage 1910 Stearns-Knight Runabout after they send the solidly frozen Boris off to the state hoosegow.

THE LAST ANGRY MOOSE

EPISODES 139–142

BULLWINKLE'S "ULTRY-SULTRY LOOK"—

plus some timely uncaged white mice – cause a group of Frostbite Falls teenage girls to faint, and that's enough to convince Bullwinkle that he's the greatest thespian since Elmo Lincoln, so he packs up his mattress – naturally, it's where he keeps his life savings – and he and Rocky are off to Hollywood to conquer the talkies!

One hundred & forty

No sooner are our heroes in Tinseltown than they run into a vaguely familiar face, but it goes with an

unfamiliar name – D.W. Grifter, World Famous Talent Scout, who immediately promises to make Bullwinkle a big star.

One hundred & forty-one

In time-honored show business fashion, the first thing

D.W. does for his new client is to change his name to Crag Antler and enroll him in the Thimblerig School of Drama and Dance, where limber-footed, Pottsylvanian-accented drama coach Gregory Ratt teaches such courses as Theoretical and Applied Mumbling. Before you can say method actor, Crag Antler, that disheveled and goateed method mumbler, has caught the eye of esteemed film director Alfred Hitchhike – who, oddly enough, also has a familiar face and a Pottsylvanian accent. Bullwinkle, that is, Crag, is on the verge of his big break.

One hundred & forty-two

Director Alfred Hitchhike's big new blockbuster, *The Last Angry Moose*, starring Crag Antler, makes Bullwinkle an overnight sensation. But "Crag"

pulls a Garbo and gives up all the glitter and glamour for the quiet life with his pal Rocky back home in little Frostbite Falls.

And now, for all you seniors who are just about to graduate, here are some words of wisdom from…

MR. KNOW-iT-ALL

Today's lecture is entitled "How to Catch a Bee…and Make Your Honey Happy." Ordinarily one can find a bee in a meadow of sweet-smelling flowers. However, if one lives in Death Valley, the task becomes a little tougher, but not insurmountable. A Geiger counter will help tell us two things: whether we are approaching a bee or walking over a land mine.

[KA–BOOM!!!!]

If the bee lover can't find the bee, make the bee come to the bee lover! This can be attained by luring him with a honeycomb. We simply take a comb, gook it up with a jar of honey.

[KA–BOOM!!!!]

You can be sure a bee will make a beeline for it!

[KA–BOOM!!!!]

Make sure, however, your bee isn't a bee twenty-nine! Moving from Death Valley to a meadow of sweet-smelling flowers, we finally do locate a bee. Utilizing the thumb and forefinger, we gently pick him up so as not to hurt his delicate little –

[KA–BOOM!!!!]

So remember next election day, when you go into the voting booth: Don't vote for Proposition Bee!

WAILING WHALE

WHOOWHOOWHA! THAT MOURNFUL WAIL

Dick. But when Parnassus takes an unexpected dive, Bullwinkle, heroic moose that he is, plunges in to save him, forgetting as he jumps just one little thing….He can't swim!

One hundred & forty-five

The quick-witted squirrel snags a crane and hooks Bullwinkle and Parnassus back up on ship. But even though the shipping magnate is sending the mighty moose and the brave flying squirrel to certain watery doom in Maybe Dick's monstrous maw, he's rather pleased with himself: Not only has he taken out big insurance policies on Rocky and Bullwinkle with himself as beneficiary, but, unbeknownst to our boys, their little vessel is loaded with dynamite as well.

One hundred & forty-six

Searching the *Atabasco,* their little vessel, Rocky and Bullwinkle follow the voice singing, "Over the Marjorie Main," and discover that none other than Captain Peter "Wrong Way" Peachfuzz is in charge. The good captain's less than thrilled to be going fishing for the mighty wailing whale.

One hundred & forty-seven

They may be hunting Maybe Dick, but Rocky's got the uneasy feeling that something's watching them. "Peeping Tom off the port bow!" sputters Captain Peachfuzz, spotting a gigantic shining eye. Rowing over to investigate, Bullwinkle's pulled under.

One hundred & forty-eight

Outfitted with scuba gear, Rocky dives to the rescue, but when neither of our heroes returns to the

surface, the entire world goes into shock, Including Peachfuzz, who takes the plunge too, leaving the S.S. *Atabasco* to sail aimlessly, adrift.

THE LEGENDARY WAILING WHALE MAYBE DICK

One hundred & forty-nine

Far below the upper deep, Peachfuzz and Rocky are snatched by a mysterious sea creature. Meanwhile, back in port, the pilotless TNT-laden little vessel, *Atabasco,* comes crashing back into Pericles Parnassus's dock and…EXPLODES!

haunting the sea lanes turns out to be…a mournful whale, Maybe Dick to be exact, maybe the biggest, baddest whale ever, and just maybe the Scourge of the Seven Seas. When shipping magnate Pericles Parnassus offers a nice little boat as reward to anyone who will fish for the dread Maybe Dick, there's not a nitwit in the world who'll take him up on his dangerous offer. Or is there?

One hundred & forty-four

It's too late for second thoughts. Rocky and Bullwinkle are shanghaied by Parnassus, the shipping magnate, who personally comes dockside to see them off on their quest for Maybe

One hundred & fifty

The crab-clawed sea monster turns out to be metallic; inside is Fiorello La Pompano, mayor of the undersea city of Submerbia, where the recently disappeared Bullwinkle currently resides.

One hundred & fifty-one

Bullwinkle and Rocky may be natives of the Land of Ten Thousand Lakes, but in the undersea city they're just two more Drylanders, until Mayor Fiorello finds out they've come to hunt Maybe Dick, who for sure is no friend of Submerbia's. In fact, a sudden sea quake turns out to be the leviathan floating past and bumping the undersea city's plastic protective dome.

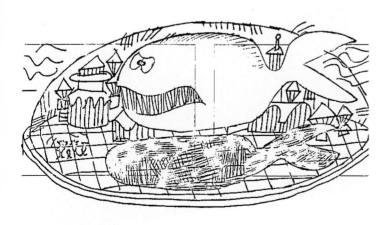

One hundred & fifty-two

Bullwinkle uses his own dome – his antlers, that is – to seal the holes in the city's dome before using his bicycle-harnessed moosle power to propel a small sub carrying him, Rocky, and Captain Peachfuzz right Into…Maybe Dick's cavernous mouth!

One hundred & fifty-three

When Rocky has a little trouble expressing his feelings upon being swallowed up by the wailing whale, Bullwinkle, lightening the situation with his usual cosmopolitan humor, suggests the flying squirrel speak in Czechoslovakian; after all, says the moose, I've always found it easy to pick up the check. Once that's straightened out, our heroes discover that the wailing whale is really a fish story, actually a disguised pirate ship. The pirate captain is a vaguely familiar menacing figure – Captain Horatio Hornswaggle – whose sidekick is an eight-foot-tall playmate-craving ape named Rollo.

One hundred & fifty-four

Rocky has a rather urgent invitation to play pat-a-cake with an eight-foot ape, but prudently he keeps declining.

One hundred & fifty-five

Captain Hornswoggle turns out to be pretty handy with a bomb, while Bullwinkle shows a natural talent for playing catch with Rollo.

One hundred & fifty-six

When Rollo knocks a bomb out of Captain Hornswoggle's hand, that's Badenov, but when the explosion comes, it's not the bomb at all, which turns out to be counterfeit, but, rather…depth charges! Fired by…an attacking squadron of British aircraft way past their tea time! Outnumbered and outgunned, Boris and Natasha make a strategic retreat to the nearest lifeboat, but affectionate Rollo, the eight-foot ape, is not to be left behind. He dives in and the boat capsizes! Meanwhile, the squadron's about to make another lethal bombing run, but…quick-witted Rocky takes to air with a painting brush, painting on the top of Maybe Dick a giant "T," which convinces the British bombers that it's their countrymen below. But it turns out the plucky squirrel wasn't trying to suggest a refreshing liquid repast, he was just starting to spell T-H-E E-N-D.

"That's an antihistamine piece of information! (i.e., it's not to be sneezed at)"

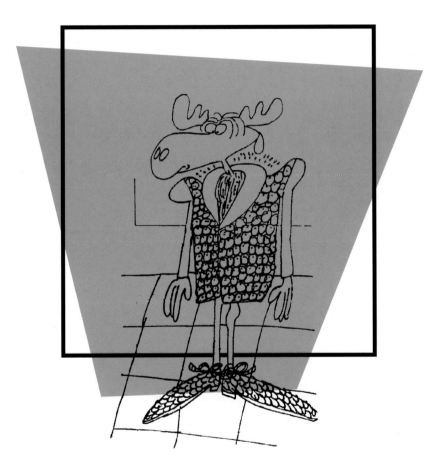

THREE MOOSEKETEERS

EPISODES 157–164

THE SMALL PROVINCE OF

Applesauce-Lorraine is favored by its natural barrier of Limburger Lillies, keeping out potential invaders (even those with sinus problems), and by a wise ruler, the good king Once-A-Louse.

But when the greedy François Villain overthrows the king, he bankrupts the kingdom with his spendthrift ways, and then institutes dread new taxes, such as the carpet and the thumb tax. Ninety-year-old former Musketeer, Athos, crotchets to the rescue, traveling to America to summon his retired compatriots, Porthos and Aramis. Inadvertently arriving in Frostbite Falls, myopic old Athos mistakes Bullwinkle's expert shish-kabob-skewering

barbecuing style for swordplay and enlists our heroes in the belief that they're really his old Musketeer comrades-in-arms.

One hundred & fifty-eight

Rocky and Bullwinkle can't resist the challenge of helping Athos rescue the citizens of Applesauce-Lorraine from the evil François Villain, so, with the aid of the *Weeders Digest,* they figure out how to breach the impregnable Limburger Lilly border. Soon Bullwinkle's way with a shish-kabob skewer has dispatched several of Villain's men, but Villain

and his archspy, Citizen Philippe Mignon, are ready with evil trickery and our would-be rescuers end up in a locked room with the walls closing in.

One hundred & fifty-nine

Bullwinkle decides to while away the time while the walls are closing in by yo-yoing. But in Applesauce-Lorraine, where the citizenry still lives as if it were the sixteenth century, a yo-yo is one of the wonders of the world. The evil François Villain trades our heroes' jobs in the scullery as cooks for the prized yo-yo. Once there, Rocky bakes a huge cake and hides Bullwinkle in it to overhear the whereabouts of the legitimate king, but the plucky squirrel may have cut things a little too thin, because the hungry François is wielding a disturbingly large cake-carving knife.

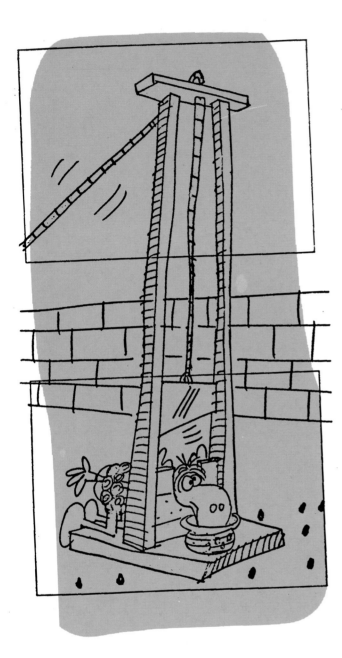

One hundred & sixty

The cake-encased moose is allergic to baking powder and the resulting mega-sneeze splatters the evil François Villain with frosting. Eventually, Bullwinkle's single-minded pursuit of the wrongfully imprisoned good king, Once-A-Louse, leads to stage center and a date with a snappy blade, but Rocky takes his pal's place under the guillotine. Has he lost his head, or is he going to?

One hundred & sixty-one

When evil François Villain is deprived of his favorite Meekly Moose cartoon on a visit to the King Theater, it's Rocky who gets it in the neck when he's thrown into the deepest dungeon under Chateau Briand. Ancient Musketeer Athos and the mighty Aramoose, his boon Mooseketeer companion, are bound and determined to rescue their plucky pal Rocky; and even though it's made of flypaper, the giant paper airplane Bullwinkle constructs for the task isn't enough to keep them from being bound and also taken prisoner.

One hundred & sixty-two

Breaking out of the dungeon, the three Mooseketeers go their separate ways, each searching for the missing monarch. In another part of Chateau Briand, Rocky finds the king, who's wearing a girdle (because François Villain didn't have an iron mask, of course). Presently, Bullwinkle turns up with *another* captive king of Applesauce-Lorraine in tow.

One hundred & sixty-three

Three kings may be swell in poker, but they're making applesauce of Rocky and Bullwinkle's plan to restore

the rightful monarch of the land of Applesauce-Lorraine, located somewhere between France and Baja, California. Fortunately, the plucky squirrel deduces from their idiosyncratic footwear that two of the three kings are impostors – actually, a track star and professional roller skater, respectively. On a stop later at the Outside Inn, our heroes learn that the evil François Villain is about to crown himself king. Will they get back in time? And do they have the right king?

One hundred & sixty-four

The coronation is under way, but Rocky and Bullwinkle have played for time by adding a few extra pages to the archbishop's coronation speech, and soon that worthy and wordy divine is declaiming bits from the Gettysburg Address, Marc Antony's funeral oration for Julius Caesar, and Lou Gehrig's farewell speech. In a last-ditch effort, Bullwinkle turns up as a traveling vacuum cleaner salesman, disrupting the proceedings with a timely demonstration that sucks up not only the crown, but the archbishop and François Villain himself. In the nick of time, Rocky appears with the rightful king of Applesauce-Lorraine.

And now time for the biggest thinker of them all...

MR. KNOW-IT-ALL

Today's mental fire drill comes under the heading

of "How to Be a Cow Puncher...without Getting Hit Back."

First, join a cattle drive, which means seeing the person who does the hiring;

namely, the fiveman, who is, of course, a foreman who got promoted. Then, attach a hot

water bottle to your gun; it is, after all, a...sick shooter. After serving his apprenticeship, the

full-fledged cowboy puts his knowledge to use by joining the rodeo or radio (both pronunciations

are correct). But when riding a bucking bronco, it is advisable that it be on a merry-go-round. So

remember: Carry a pocketful of dimes!

LAZY JAY RANCH

EPISODES 165–182

IT WASN'T JUST TV-WATCHING

fifties America that was nuts about westerns, the craze even got to Bullwinkle, too.

One hundred & sixty-five

Bullwinkle so loves watching *Two-Gun Twombley*, his favorite TV western, that he's gone cowboy happy, even roping the morning milk in off the front porch and watching TV from his very own saddle. Rocky tries to get his pal to cut off his out-of-control western-watching by limiting the quick-draw-happy moose to shows like *Ding Dong School* and *Meet the Press*, but when Bullwinkle inadvertently blows up the set, he's reduced to reading – *Raunchy Ranch Tales*,

Cowhand Comics, *Side Saddle Stories*, and the like – until he chances upon an ad in the newspaper: FOR SALE, the Lazy Jay Ranch in Squaws Ankle, Wyoming, only twenty-eight dollars.

One hundred & sixty-six

Perhaps if our heroes had realized that a monster was ravaging Squaws Ankle, they might've questioned why the Lazy Jay spread was such a bargain, instead of just buying it.

One hundred & sixty-seven

On the way to the Lazy Jay, Bullwinkle gets the point when he takes a fall right onto a prickly cactus, but our heroes are really on pins and needles when Lazy Jay himself starts taking potshots at them. But Jay's really too lazy to

keep at it, so he gives the new owners a tour of the ranch's points of interest, such as Dead Man's Swamp, Grizzly Gulch, and the Burning Bandlands.

One hundred & sixty-eight

They don't raise cows at the Lazy Jay, nope, or steers, or sheep, or chinchillas or horses neither,

partner. When the bespectacled eponymous former owner whispers what they *do* raise to our two heroes, they both faint dead away, for the Lazy Jay is a worm ranch. *But* they get over it, and a pogoing Rocky and Bullwinkle are soon rounding up the worm herd, watched surreptitiously by a sinister figure in a cowboy hat and kilts – that vaguely familiar-looking Scottish cowboy, Black Angus.

One hundred & sixty-nine

Ever optimistic, Rocky decides to make a going concern out of the Lazy Jay by selling the rocks he's clearing away from the North Forty, but the pile just keeps getting bigger and bigger until he hits on the idea of putting a WARNING: DO NOT TAKE ROCKS sign up. All the rocks are promptly stolen by Boris and Natasha, who proceed to set a huge boulder rolling in the direction of hapless Squaws Ankle.

One hundred & seventy

The huge boulder crashes into the Squaws Ankle assay office, which just happens to be where Boris and Natasha have taken shelter. Assaying the debris of the boulder, Boris is moved to perform

an impromptu assay with his handy Stolen Metals Analyzer, and he discovers that the Lazy Jay Ranch contains a fortune in practically every known precious metal, from gold to molybdenum. Meanwhile, Rocky and Bullwinkle are finishing up the spring worm roundup (all that branding is the tough part).

One hundred & seventy-one

Black Angus, the Scottish cowpoke, and Natasha "Lavish" MacTavish, the spendthrift Scot, sign on as cowhands for the Lazy Jay worm-herd drive to a fishing resort fifty miles away.

One hundred & seventy-two

Boris and Natasha's Fiendish Plan is to drive the worm herd over a cliff and thereby ruin the Lazy Jay so they can buy it up cheap. But they're foiled when the ingenious little worm critters, part silkworms after all, spin little parachutes on the way down. The result: forty thousand silk handkerchiefs, enough for all of Bullwinkle's Christmas shopping!

One hundred & seventy-three

Boris takes umbrage at being told what to do, so he tears up the script, causing a momentary confusion of line reading, but our heroes drive the

worm herd on toward the Angels Cramp fishing resort anyhow, with TV-western-lover Bullwinkle singing a hearty chorus of "Head 'em up, Move 'em out, Medium-rare hide." Pasting the script back together to find out what the Fiendish Plan is,

Boris then quickly leafs through his *Disguises for All Occasions* book, settling on impersonating the terrible Wutzat monster.

One hundred & seventy-four

Rocky and Bullwinkle are pretty spooked by the fake Wutzat, which really is just Boris and Natasha

in disguise. But the dastardly duo's victory is short-lived, because they themselves are soon pursued by the *real* Wutzat, who turns out not to be extinct after all.

One hundred & seventy-five

A real crisis is drowning that angler's paradise, wonderful Wyoming, for right there, in that

fabulous fishing resort, Angels Cramp, there are thousands of fish, and thousands of fishermen, but absolutely no bait! If Bullwinkle and Rocky can drive their worm herd into camp in time, they'll be millionaires! But Boris and Natasha have other plans.

One hundred & seventy-six

Consulting the *Fireside Crook Book*, Boris dons Indian gear to perform a rain dance, which will result in a cloudburst, which then will soak the parched ground, which will give the worms a chill that turns into pneumonia – achoo! and they're gone. There's only one little problem: Boris's terpsichorean gyrations don't produce a drop of moisture, so the saturnine spy does the obvious: He washes his vintage Essex auto, and – *KA-POW!* – lightning flashes and thunder roars, and the desert turns into a flooded lake!

One hundred & seventy-seven

Just as our heroes have at last wrangled the worm herd into Angels Cramp fishing resort, an inopportune lightning strike turns every last wriggler into a glowworm, rendering them useless as bait. Unflappable Bullwinkle points out that the only thing better as bait than angleworms is the rare and hard-to-pick finkleberry, a bush of which just happens to be nearby. Rocky immediately alley-oops into the air, certain he can corral the reticent berries, but it's an open question if cocky Rocky will pick a peck of finkleberries or not.

One hundred & seventy-eight

So irresistible are the fine finkleberries to the finny fish that the Angels Cramp fishing resort is soon awash with eager anglers' money. Naturally, Rocky and Bullwinkle drive the fishy fortune to the bank in nearby Squaws Ankle, Wyoming, but Bullwinkle manages to steer their turret-topped armored car directly into Boris and Natasha's rain-dance-created lake.

One hundred & seventy-nine

While Boris and Natasha depth-charge the armored car from above, Rocky rescues the money and – like some furry, underwater-launched guided missile – shoots out of the armored car's cannon.

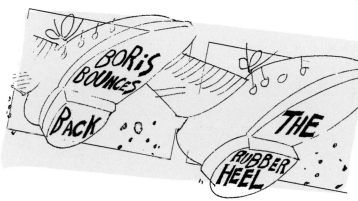

When their little boat gets picked up by the armored car Bullwinkle is busily driving, Boris finds the silver lining – There's a little bad in everything good that happens, says he to Natasha – just before a low bridge gives them the big brushoff.

One hundred & eighty

Our heroes have the money safely deposited in the Hogbreeders National Bank in Squaws Ankle, but two vaguely familiar faces suddenly show up, proclaiming themselves to be that famous electric company detective, Sherlock Ohms, and his assistant, Doctor Watts, dollink.

One hundred & eighty-one

It's bank night for bank robbers in little Squaws Ankle, Wyoming, where Boris has just cut the main power line leading into town, leaving every vault, cash register, and safe open and defenseless, and keeping the citizenry in the dark, until Rocky has a brilliant flash: Use their Lazy Jay Ranch glowworm herd to light up the night!

One hundred & eighty-two

Things have certainly brightened in Squaws Ankle, thanks to Rocky's brilliant use of the glowworms to light up the town and foil Boris and Natasha's

scheme to rob it in the dark. In fact, when the glowworms decide to remain at their posts, Squaws Ankle becomes a colorful tourist destination and the grateful mayor plans to rename it Squirrels Ankle, Wyoming. Not entirely everyone is completely delighted, however, and Boris plans a twenty-million-volt hotfoot when our heroes' train rolls by. Will it be roast moose and squirrel fricassee? When Boris and Natasha – each holding an electric power cable – shake on it, they make an unwanted connection, lighting up like a juice-jangled pinball machine, and our heroes, their cowboy craze satisfied, head off into the sunset, on their way back to Frostbite Falls.

"There's nobody as stupid as the hero of a TV cartoon show."
(Article Six, <u>Villains Handbook</u>)

MISSOURI MISHMASH

THERE'S EXCITEMENT IN

placid Frostbite Falls, Minnesota, when an actual telegram arrives for Bullwinkle J. Moose, inviting him to the annual BAMBAMS convention – the Big American Mooses Benevolent Artistic and Marching Society, that is – in Peaceful Valley, Missouri. But as our impecunious heroes walk the railroad tracks between Minnesota and Missouri, they're being watched by a satellite eye-in-the-sky, broadcasting their every move to the sinister Fearless Leader.

One hundred & eighty-four

Boris is rolling a huge boulder straight down the hill at our friends, innocently strolling the railroad

tracks, when a buzzard – that is, a Pottsylvanian carrier pigeon – arrives with a message from Fearless Leader:

Moose and Squirrel must make it safely to Peaceful Valley.

MOOSE AND SQUIRREL MUST ARRIVE AT PEACEFUL VALLEY SAFE AND SOUND *fearless leader*

One hundred & eighty-five

Boris gets hammered so hard by his own runaway boulder that he not only forgets who Fearless Leader is, he actually forgets that he's supposed to be mean.

One hundred & eighty-six

Due to a serious bonk on the noggin, Boris has reformed, promising never to do anything that that meanie Fearless Leader orders, and since Fearless Leader's last order was *don't* kill Moose and Squirrel, to Boris's twisted way of thinking that

means blow 'em up now! But the eye-in-the-sky is still watching, and at Fearless Leader's command, a door in the satellite opens, and a hand appears and drops a brick right on Boris's head, hundreds of miles below. The resulting explosion blows our heroes free and conks Boris back to abnormal.

One hundred & eighty-seven

Protecting Moose and Squirrel is all part of the plot, says Fearless Leader, pointing out that in the immortal words of Mister Big, a watched plot never thickens. But a watched Boris does get his satellite marching orders, while Natasha goes through her pocketbook in search of a Secret Agent Pocket Kit, but all she can find is poison lipstick in kiss-of-death pink, some booby pins for setting booby traps, an autographed picture of Benedict Arnold, and her PTA membership card (that is, Pickpockets and Thieves Associated, of course). Meanwhile, in search of some cooling shade, our heroes enter a nice cool tunnel, only to come racing out pursued by a fast express train that lands them right back where they started, in Frostbite Falls.

One hundred & eighty-eight

To get to Peaceful Valley, Rocky and Bullwinkle are going to need a demon travel agent, and that's exactly who they get when a vaguely familiar Tradewind La Tour turns up, with a trip itinerary that includes stops in Paris, Greenland, Nome, and Pismo Beach. But our heroes don't have the ten-thousand-dollar tariff; their thirty-eight cents total does buy an alternate itinerary – namely, straight down the Missouri River via the S.S. *Huck Finn*, a rather small raft. Meanwhile, Boris pursues in the lap of luxury, reclining in a rickshaw pulled by Natasha, who, Boris blithely assures her, will have a figure like M.M. by the end of their journey. Marilyn Monroe? inquires Ms. Fatale. Not at all, replies Boris. Minnie Mouse.

One hundred & eighty-nine

At last arriving in Peaceful Valley, Missouri, our heroes find the town deserted, but that's only because two feuding clans, the Hatfuls and the Floys, are about to start blasting from opposite sides of the main street.

One hundred & ninety

Taken prisoner by the Hatfuls, Rocky and Bullwinkle are taken at gunpoint to their leader,

Hateful Dan Hatful, who turns out to be Boris in a fake beard. Meanwhile, Fearless Leader boards a sleek black missile for the express flight to Peaceful Valley.

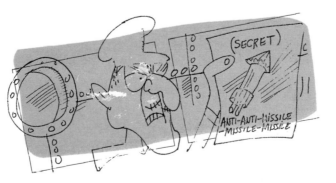

One hundred & ninety-one

So eager is Fearless Leader to take charge from Boris Badenov in Peaceful Valley that he makes the trip by orbital rocket. The only complication: Pottsylvania doesn't have the technology to get him down. While Fearless Leader threatens and blusters, good Samaritan Rocky takes action, alley-ooping into orbit to rescue his nemesis, who, mistaking the fearless squirrel for an American anti-missile-missile, unveils his own counter-weapon – the dread anti-anti-missile-missile-missile!

One hundred & ninety-two

Rocky is slowing the misguided missile, while inside Fearless Leader is assembling his top-secret anti-anti-missile-missile-missile from a kit he got out of a cereal box. Just as Fearless fires, gallant TV hero Rocky dives downward to help a little old lady – who looks very much like a certain Pottsyl-vanian spy with ambitions to become the new

Fearless Leader – cross the street. However, back on the missile, the recoil from the weapon's misfire sends Fearless Leader crashing to earth just in time for phase two of his dastardly plan to unfold, so, as peacemakers Rocky and Bullwinkle head off to the cabin of feuding paterfamilias Felonious Floy, Boris and a brace of moose-hunting dogs are in hot pursuit.

One hundred & ninety-three

REVENOOERS AND REPUBLICANS KEEP OUT says the welcoming sign in front of Felonious Floy's mountain cabin, but when the Floy boy himself appears at the door with a shotgun and a strong resemblance to Boris Badenov, he gives our heroes the ol' trapdoor routine. A grateful Fearless Leader then gives Boris the Pottsylvanian Two-Faced Medal for being on both sides of the Hatful-Floy feud. Meanwhile, the hateful Hatfuls have the Floy cabin surrounded and are bringing up Little Orvie, an enormous Civil War cannon. Just as the fuse is lit, Bullwinkle pops up from the root cellar where he and Rocky had fallen, right in front of the cannon's mouth.

One hundred & ninety-four

Unaware of the imminent big blast from Little Orvie, inside the Floy cabin Fearless Leader

explains to Boris that soon they'll have the ultimate weapon – namely, the Kerward Derby, a fabulous bowler that makes its wearer the smartest person on earth, but can be located only by the stupidest bubblehead in the world, and that's exactly why Boris must keep Bullwinkle safe at any cost.

One hundred & ninety-five

KA–BOOM! Little Orvie explodes, blowing the Floy cabin up and sending everyone but Rocky and Bullwinkle, who were safe in the root cellar, flying. Rocky and Bullwinkle might not be out of danger yet, but they are out of the picture, having suddenly disappeared.

One hundred & ninety-six

It's a touching moment all right when Boris and Fearless Leader sing a few bars of the Pottsylvanian National Anthem: *Hail, hail, Pottsylvania, hail to the black and the blue / Hail, hail, Pottsylvania, sneaky and crooked through and through / Down with the good guys, up with the bad, under the sign of the Triple Cross / Hail, hail, hail!* Meanwhile, the feuding Hatful clan has captured Bullwinkle, who's being carried in the direction of an ominous–looking torture chamber, while Rocky braves squirrel guns to chase after them.

One hundred & ninety-seven

A brainwash to Bullwinkle has no more effect than a nice shampoo. So Boris and Fearless Leader resort to the Beautiful Dreamer Hypnotism Kit to mesmerize the moose into finding the sensational

chapeau. Meanwhile, Rocky has succeeded in freeing himself from the Hatful clan trap and follows Bullwinkle's antler scrapes on passing trees all the way to a sinister cottage deep in the woods, but no one's home.

One hundred & ninety-eight

The mesmerized moose is leading Fearless and Boris on quite a bowler tour – the Brown Derby, the Kentucky Derby, and even the Roller Derby – but so

far no sign of the fabulous Kerward Derby. So when Rocky turns up, Boris and Fearless Leader fearlessly take a powder, after first implanting a posthypnotic suggestion: Find the Kerward Derby! *Snap,* and Bullwinkle is driven to go to the nearest hat store, where, on a long-forgotten dusty shelf, a clerk finds one chapeau in exactly the moose's seven and five thirty-seconds hat size.

One hundred & ninety-nine

Bullwinkle puts on the Kerward Derby and becomes the smartest person in the world, able to foil Boris's battle-ax attack through sheer brain power and to speak in perfect *français.*

Two hundred

Just as Bullwinkle's about to explain Einstein's Theory of Relativity to Rocky, a stray breath of wind blows the bowler off his antlered brow. Boris quickly steals the real derby, leaving behind a similar bowler with a time bomb inside, which Bullwinkle immediately dons.

Two hundred & one

Boris, Natasha, and Fearless Leader all have set to squabbling over possession of the real Kerward Derby, which goes rolling right into our heroes' hands, while the bogus, time-bomb-filled bowler ends up on Boris's head. The resulting explosion brings the baddies back together again.

Two hundred & two

Our heroes keep boomeranging the derby back and forth with Boris and Natasha as they race toward Washington, D.C., where they patriotically plan to deliver

the hard-fought-over hat to the head of government, but they run into the bureaucracy instead.

Two hundred & three

Rocky and Bullwinkle are escorted through Washington by none other than official greeter Hailfellow J. Backslap ("Jay" Backslap, get it?), a vaguely familiar face whose welcome is waggin', for he leads our heroes to the ramshackle and sinister Little White House, where the president is waiting, the president of the Liquidate Rocky and Bullwinkle Club, that is.

Two hundred & four

Everybody wants the fabulous Kerward Derby, including Gidney and Cloyd, those two scrooch-gun-wielding moon men, who need

it for their king, Nosmo the One-Halfth, child of King Ughbert the Ugly and Queen Ethelred the Unready, who is a dimwitted moon mis-prince in need of smartening-up.

Two hundred & five

Cloyd and Gidney relate their looney – ahem, lunar – tale: The moon wizard had labored mightily to brighten up Nosmo the One-Halfth, but instead of creating a crown fit for a moon king, the wizard - a fellow by the name of Kerward – came up with the derby. The Kerward Derby was only lent to them on their previous visit, the moon men add, and they'd misplaced it.

Two hundred & six

Fearless Leader is lying in wait, machine gun at the ready, until he's scrooched into immobility by Cloyd and Gidney. Meanwhile, Boris, disguised as an official Washington greeter, escorts our heroes right into the Potomac before making off with the bountiful bowler.

Two hundred & seven

No sooner does baddie Boris pop on the bowler than he discovers that crime really *doesn't* pay; in disgust, he hurls it out the window and right into the waiting arms of the two moon men. Meanwhile, considering how many nuts there are in Congress, nobody, including our heroes, seems surprised to learn that the new congressman from a small town in Missouri is…Rocket J. Squirrel, whose first task it is to untangle the furiously feuding Hatful and Floy clans.

Two hundred & eight

Rocky's one squirrel who knows how to get all his nuts in order: Cloyd and Gidney return to the moon with their derby, Boris and Natasha are foiled, and, with a little help from a certain moose, Congressman R. J. Squirrel makes his maiden speech.

TOPSY TURVY

EPISODES 209–222

HOKEY SMOKE!

The weather in Frostbite Falls is sure peculiar this April! Instead of the usual touch of frostbite in the air in Frostbite, the sun is actually shining, and a dilly of a daffodil is already in bloom! Could the weather actually be changing? The hibernating bears will tell, Rocky realizes, but when Bullwinkle helpfully points out the Hibernian right there on the street, the citizens go a-shrieking away! When Rocky tries to get the weather report from the newspaper, the sweet-tempered squirrel is incensed to learn that the weather report has been classified for the duration of the emergency period. Or is that emergency, period? Bullwinkle prudently inquires, so our heroes rush to the town library to read up on the subject of the suddenly sunny local weather, but along with the volumes in the stacks is a pair of beady eyes.

Two hundred & ten

Is that beady-eyed, Bogartish kinda guy with the gun on 'im the librarian perhaps? our heroes hopefully surmise, or maybe a refugee from some other TV show, some gritty crime drama? Whichever… he's got them at gunpoint and is marching them right through the center of town, which surprises the always-helpful townsfolk who hadn't realized it was moose- and squirrel-hunting season. The agent takes them to his chief, who turns out to be their old pal, the wrong-way expert, Captain Peachfuzz himself, who informs our friends that even the word W-H-E-T-H-E-R has been classified. But when Rocky corrects the good captain about his spelling, Peachfuzz immediately concludes that our heroes already know what the agent has been trying to keep hush-hush (or perhaps that's actually spelled 'ush-'ush?), namely, that the weather – and the world – is turning upside down!

Two hundred & eleven

Those two learned polymaths, Professor Werner Von Beige and Captain Peter "Wrong Way" Peachfuzz, explain exactly why the earth has turned upside down: It seems that the North Pole has become top-heavy with ice and "slipped" down into the West Pacific; that puts Frostbite Falls on the equator and Chicago where Honolulu used to be. Naturally, Von Beige's fellow scientists think he's inverted his toupee – flipped his lid, that is – until California is flooded and, ahem, Disneyland has to be evacuated.

Two hundred & twelve

It's backward to the new West Pole with Captain Peachfuzz at the controls and enough heating pads and snaps of Lola Lollapolooza along to melt things back to normal, but before you can say Wrong Way! the plane goes down and our heroes parachute back to the airport, where, because it's a fantasy show, they can afford to pick up another aircraft immediately. This time it's Rocket J. Squirrel himself at the controls! But because it's a long journey (Clock hands spin, leaves fall, calendar pages blow away in the breeze!), they run out of gas, thereby, Bullwinkle proudly points out, setting a new record: crashing two planes in one episode! Whether a plane or FM radio, Bullwinkle disdains to use it to call for help; after all, they *are* TV people, aren't they? But so desperate is the situation that it's even too late for jokes!

Two hundred & thirteen

They're going down for sure, until Rocky happens upon a copy of the *Congressional Record*. As Bullwinkle reads passages from it into the jet's fuel system, the blast of hot air propels them onward! In fact, that one single volume of the *Congressional Record* contains enough hot air to power a four-engine jet plane all the way around the world.

Two hundred & fourteen

Bullwinkle's stirring reading of the *Congressional Record* has put everyone within hearing distance, including our Narrator, to sleep, so no one knows where anyone is until the professor consults the aircraft window to see right below them…a little tropical island, the new North Pole. At that moment, on the island, the natives are preparing a warm welcome for our heroes under the direction of their Pottsylvanian-accented chief, Colonel Oglethorpe Peachtree and his vampy assistant, Magnolia Blossom – two names that are appropriate, says Boris, because it is, after all, the *South*

black cooking pot, as Bullwinkle parachutes toward a swamp filled with ravenous moose-eating crocodiles.

Pacific. Meanwhile, aboard the jet, our heroes are discussing the well-known fact that the Riki Tiki natives are friendly and harmless, when bombs explode all about them and they're forced to bail out. No, they're not sinking, but they are floating rapidly down toward the spear-brandishing cannibals below.

Two hundred & fifteen

Colonel Peachtree dispatches Howard and Emery, two fierce-looking hawks with stainless steel beaks and poison-tipped talons, to dispatch our heroes, but not before he informs Natasha – that is, "Magnolia" – that the birds didn't come from an agent, he got them from a...*talon* scout.

Two hundred & sixteen

As the ice-laden North Pole tips farther down in the Pacific, it's only a matter of time until the island of Riki-Tiki becomes the new North Pole, or so figures Boris Badenov, who tells Natasha that he plans to become the new Santa Claus.

Two hundred & seventeen

Boris Claus is going to turn Christmas into the biggest inside job ever, coming down the chimney

armed and larcenous and using reindeer and sleigh to move the loot. Meanwhile, a dazed Rocket J. is sailing directly toward a group of fierce natives with spears, cookbooks, and a big

Two hundred & eighteen

The natives have Rocky in a pretty stew all right, until they see what a sweet guy he is and decide they're going to have him for dessert instead. Yes, Rocky really would be in hot water if not for the sudden appearance of the Great Swamp Spirit, who stampedes the natives. Actually it's Bullwinkle staggering through the jungle with a parachute tangled around his head. But before our heroes can make their getaway, Riki-Tiki ticks north again and the temperature drops precipitously.

Two-hundred & nineteen

The natives' Rocky stew has frozen solid, with our hero stuck in the middle of the pot, until Bullwinkle takes a quick trip, knocks the pot over, and leaves Rocky on a pile of cubes, a sort of Rocky-on-the-rocks.

Two hundred & twenty

Boris shows up in his Sandy Claus costume, with his tall elf assistant, Alf, by his side and in his bag a *tick-tick-ticking* present for Bullwinkle J. Moose.

Two hundred & twenty-one

Boris Claus is bound to get a jolt out of the present that good-hearted Bullwinkle tosses in the back of his sleigh: It's the rewrapped time bomb that Boris originally had given to the Moose!

Meanwhile, teeth-chattering natives figure a moose coat with a squirrel collar is just the thing to deal with their new status as the Riki-Tiki North Pole.

Two hundred & twenty-two

They don't call him "Wrong Way" for nothing: Captain Peachfuzz saves the day when the boxes of trinkets he'd brought along to trade with the tropical natives turn out to contain warm

winter clothes instead. Meanwhile, Rocky hits on the perfect TV-hero solution to turning the world the right way: a television telethon, soliciting worldwide contributions of snow. Those, and a little flying-squirrel cloud-seeding, flip the world right back over to where it belongs. As for Boris Claus, he gets a real bang out of Bullwinkle's gift.

And here he is with an open mind and a hole in his head to prove it...

MR. KNOW-IT-ALL

Today's lecture is "How to Be an Archeologist... and Dig Ancient History."

The archeologist must have a thorough knowledge of his subject, which is, uh...um, Archeology! I have even gone so far as to read a book on it: *Desire Under the Sphinx.* To practice archeology, we must travel to places that are famous for old relics, such as Pasadena... or even Egypt...where Abu Ben Boris will gladly show you the pyramids, and where the walls are covered with ancient hiero-glyphics, but don't worry, with a little cleanser and some elbow grease, they'll come right off.

Here's an interesting speci-men: It translates as Pharaoh Loves Zelda!

Painting Theft

Episodes 223–228

TWO OF THE HONEST, TRUE-BLUE, EVER-TRUSTING GUARDS

at the French National Gallery look suspiciously familiar. Yes, Boris and Natasha steal ten Old Master paintings and, to avoid being caught by the gendarmes, mail them to a certain moose in a certain Minnesota hamlet. When the parcel arrives, Bullwinkle naturally assumes it's the wallpaper he'd ordered for decorating the chicken coop.

Two hundred & twenty-four

Rocky's helping Bullwinkle choose from among chicken-coop wallpaper patterns: Lessee, there's the Mona Lisa, the Laughing Cavalier....After Bullwinkle hangs the art, the hens become critics, refusing to lay. Just as Bullwinkle sets off in search of a bucket of whitewash to cover the offending artwork, the world's greatest art collector, Cerulean Bleu, and his secretary, Rose Madder, pull up in a big black limousine.

Two hundred & twenty-five

Boris – that is, Cerulean – is prepared to go as high as three ninety-eight per picture, even after Bullwinkle's covered every square inch of every Old Master with ol' Wite-Out.

Two hundred & twenty-six

Encouraged by Cerulean Bleu's magnificent offer, Bullwinkle goes into the whitewashed-painting business, turning out canvases that attract more flies than buyers. Art critics from all over are converging on little Frostbite Falls, and the bidding for Bullwinkle's masterworks is frenzied. Before you can say "Fiendish Plan," that famous artmoose Bullwinkle is accosted by a vaguely familiar-looking little boy with a rather pronounced moustache, who gets the big moose's "autograph" – right on the dotted line of Bullwinkle's Last Will and Testament, leaving his paintings to Boris Badenov.

Two hundred & twenty-seven

Bullwinkle's the art world's latest avant-garde sensation with his series of whitewashed

canvases, which Boris purchases for big bucks just before the moose's booby-trapped studio goes up with a big boom.

Two hundred & twenty-eight

With their paintings in tow, Boris and Natasha have summoned a Pottsylvanian submarine to meet them near the Pigeon River. While Boris and Natasha sail to their grim little homeland with their paintings, Bullwinkle's acclaimed whitewash series is being hung in the French National Gallery, right in the spots vacated by the stolen Old Masters. When the whitewash series is cleaned, the Old Masters are discovered back where they belong. Meanwhile, back in the art world, whitewash is passé; the new sensation is Jackson Plop, who paints with a mixture of Pablum and chicken gizzards. It looks like Bullwinkle's going to be

stuck with four thousand gallons of whitewash, until he hits on a happy solution: He sells it to the fellahs investigating payola.

THE GUNS OF ABALONE

EPISODES 229–232

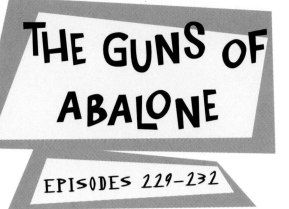

HAVING STAMPEDED RIGHT OVER

the TV western craze, Rocky and Bullwinkle now scale the heights of the World War II action-adventure in this parody of *The Guns of Navarone*.

Two hundred & twenty-nine

Our story opens with a flashback to a daring World War II commando operation to silence the massive guns of Abalone, a small island in the Aegean Sea. The guns were bombarding targets all over the globe. Now they've begun firing again and the call has gone out for volunteers to silence them once more. When a reporter overhears Bullwinkle telling Rocky he'll gladly volunteer to go to the store for milk, one thing leads to another, and soon our heroes are on a jet bound for Europe, where, on a certain Aegean island, a certain dastardly duo is preparing an explosive welcome.

Two hundred & thirty

A blast from the guns of Abalone hits Rocky and Bullwinkle's plane and they crash on the Rock of Gibraltar, where a mightily peeved British general – who takes severe umbrage when Bullwinkle suggests he put a little English on his snooker ball – claps our heroes into the local dungeon – in fact, the same one from which the Count of Monte Cristo once escaped. Well, Bullwinkle's two favorite words are es-cape, so he and Rocky tunnel out. But it's not freedom they find. It's a waiting firing squad.

Two hundred & thirty-one

The British Constitution is firm on the subject of granting the last request of a condemned moose and squirrel, so – since our heroes sensibly ask not to be shot – the British officer in charge of the firing squad has no choice but to give out pardons and put our boys aboard the first boat to Bayonne, New Jersey, which promptly goes down in a sudden squall. After all, what do you expect when you open the porthole to cool down a warm engine room?

Two hundred & thirty-two

The good ship *Lollipop* goes down, but all hands aboard board a long ship and ride out the storm under Rocky's able command, eventually coming ashore on the sands of Abalone. Fortunately a crewman had remembered to pack an alarm clock and TNT when abandoning ship, so Rocky and Bullwinkle, armed with their home-made time bomb, set off – through nooks and crannies, over smiths and dales, creeping and crawling, inching their way ever closer to the gigantic guns of Abalone. When Boris trains all of the huge guns on our heroes, who've managed to misplace their bomb, he inadvertently aims the guns of Abalone right at each other and succeeds only in blowing them all up. Rocky and Bullwinkle return in triumph to Frostbite Falls, exhausted after their trying ordeal, and immediately take to bed, but not before Bullwinkle sets a suspiciously ticking alarm clock.

Tick! Tick! Tock! Tick! Tick!

"Eenie, meenie, chili beanie, the spirits are about to speak!"

THE TREASURE OF MONTE ZOOM

EPISODES 233-240

AT THE BOTTOM OF

placid Lake Salle de Bain, near bucolic Frostbite Falls, Minnesota, "X" marks the spot where the fabulous treasure of Monte Zoom – the race car driver, that is, not the old Indian – is buried, so, natch, Boris and Natasha are about to blow up the dam. Meanwhile, our heroes, charter members of the Frostbite Falls Birdwatching and Pinochle Society, are out watching birds, with Rocky writing down all the birds that Bullwinkle, through his binoculars, espies: In addition to the tufted titmouse, there's a pair of big-nosed fuselighters. But will Bullwinkle desert his birdwatching post just to foil Boris's dam plan?

Two hundred & thirty-four

It's Rocky and Bullwinkle to the rescue, but Boris is ready for just that with his fatal Dreamsville Moose Horn and a squirrel gun, only the horn calls ducks and the gun shoots – *POP!* – an American flag – all because violence is no longer allowed on television, Natasha observes sadly. But Boris, realizing that there's a plug he can pull at the bottom of the lake, has another Fiendish Plan at the end of his line: He turns up in a Hemingwayesque Old-Man-and-the-Sea costume, proclaiming himself to be famous film actor Spencer Traceback in need of some timely moose-muscled assistance to land the Big One.

Two hundred & thirty-five

Bullwinkle doesn't know if the tuna is bluefin or piano, but it sure is one heavy fish. Little does he realize he's helping Boris drain Lake Salle de Bain to uncover the buried chest holding the fabulous treasure of Monte Zoom. When Boris pushes him over the side, Bullwinkle's sucked down the drain, through the Frostbite Falls water system and halfway out some unfortunate apartment dweller's steaming shower.

Two hundred & thirty-six

The quick-witted citizen, having turned the water up full blast, Bullwinkle pops out of the showerhead, followed presently by a flying squirrel whose goggles are seriously steamed up. Quickly

commandeering a bicycle built for two, our heroes pedal full-speed back to the now-dry lake, arriving at the scene of the once and future crime just in time for Boris to drop the weighty treasure chest right on their heads.

Two hundred & thirty-seven

Boris's scissors are a little rusty, so Natasha contributes her snap-open switchblade nail file; Rocky sees the imminent danger, but Bullwinkle

won't spring away. Is he frozen with fright? No, he's just standing on his own foot - and not the same way everybody else does either! Once the big moose has hopped to, the treasure chest plunges down with Boris atop it. When it lands atop *him,* it's little consolation to an aching Boris that it's just TV cartoon violence. Luckily, our heroes overhear Boris vowing to open the chest containing the treasure with an A-bomb, which, Bullwinkle observes dryly, is exactly what some people call their show. I don't think that's very funny, Rocky harrumphs. Neither do they, apparently, ripostes the airily persiflaging moose.

Two hundred & thirty-eight

They've hammered it, they've chopped it, they've blown it up, and even dropped it off a cliff, all to no avail. The treasure chest is impenetrable – until, that is, Bullwinkle suggests trying the key.

Ta-da! It works! Inside they find a 1903 Epperson Jackrabbit, a classic automobile. After our heroes have driven off, Boris and Natasha, unable to find an A-bomb anywhere, return, dejected, prepared to return to their regular jobs breaking windows at the United Nations building – until Boris intimidates the Narrator into revealing that the car is solid gold. Then the villains hop right after the fourteen-carat Jackrabbit.

Two hundred & thirty-nine

On the road to Frostbite Falls in their 1903 Epperson Jackrabbit, Rocky and Bullwinkle come upon the used car dealership of the Laughing Latvian, Madman Morris, who magnanimously offers them thirty bountiful bucks to take the Jackrabbit off their hands. Bullwinkle is moved to medical humor, pronouncing the Laughing Latvian's offer to be antihistamine money – nothing to sneeze at, that is. And when Madman Morris generously throws in two all-day suckers, he has himself a deal, so he and Natasha hurriedly drive off, leaving Rocky and Bullwinkle to wonder where the two suckers are. Answer's obvious, isn't it?

Two hundred & forty

The Jackrabbit turns out to be a turkey after all, as Boris and Natasha learn from Andy Grift, the neighborhood stolen-property fence, who informs them that the car is made of tin. Rocky, in true heroic form, has to fly through the flaming bridge over Buzzard's Gulch in hot pursuit of the fleeing Boris and Natasha, who, too late, discover that the true treasure of Monte Zoom is a trunk full of gold coins. Nonetheless – car, coins, and all – they go over the edge of the gulch. Bullwinkle – a self-assured moose as always – takes their happy cartoon ending for granted, until he obliviously walks over the cliff edge himself. Clinging precariously to a branch growing from the rock face, he realizes that an unhappy ending must mean that this is one of them newfangled *adult* cartoons.

GOOF-GAS ATTACK

EPISODES 241–248

THE GREATEST MINDS IN AMERICA,

himself on the electric third rail. All this has Rocky worried, and naturally Bullwinkle figures that's because the show's ratings are down again, so he assures his pal that despite all the recent attempts on his life, they're certain to be renewed. Heck, they're already in McKeesport, Pennsylvania, aren't they?

Two hundred & forty-three

Contacting Boris via two-way wrist television (Dick Tracy and all the best cartoon characters have them, doncha know?), Fearless Leader orders him to put the dread Plan X into effect. Meanwhile, it's Captain Peter "Wrong Way" Peachfuzz stepping out of the jet-plane escape pod that lands near Rocky and Bullwinkle's Washington-bound train. As for the good captain's jet, even now it's loop-de-looping down on top of them.

Two hundred & forty-four

Neatly dodging the diving jet, our heroes are just about to find out from Captain Peachfuzz why it was important for them all to meet in McKeesport, Pennsylvania, when, suddenly, he too is struck by the addlepating malady and rushes away to watch *Ding Dong School* on a nearby TV set.

Two hundred & forty-five

While Peachfuzz blithers in front of the set, our heroes set off on the track of mysterious foot-prints, mainly because good guys *always* follow mysterious footprints. At the other end of the trail, Boris waits with a goof-gas gun,

the erudite professors at the Double Dome Institute for Advanced Thinking, where even the janitor has a Ph.D. from Cal Tech, have turned into gibbering idiots, and highbrows everywhere are becoming knotheads, so in desperation, at the highest levels of government, the search is on for the biggest nitwit in the entire country to come to the rescue. But will Bullwinkle get to Washington, or will the live hand grenade hurled through his kitchen window get him first?

Two hundred & forty-two

Boris is setting a new one-episode record for failed attempts on Moose's life – first, Boris is blown up by his own hand grenade, then a booby–trapped shotgun blasts him instead, and finally – trying to derail our heroes' train – he fries

product of a secret Pottsylvanian plot to develop the ultimate weapon and turn it against every other country in the world, beginning with the easiest target, the U.S. of A.

Two hundred & forty-six

Kaff–kaff–kaff! Boris launches his goof-gas attack, making Rocky extremely forgetful (he's even forgotten what it was that he forgot), but leaving Bullwinkle unchanged. No brain, no effect, says Boris with a shrug, going with Natasha to Washington, D.C. and the Congressional Visitors Gallery, where listening to a few intemperate speeches convinces him that a goof-gas attack here would be redundant, so he gases the Narrator instead, who promptly forgets what the next episode is about.

Two hundred & forty-seven

Boris and Natasha have taken their goof-gas attack south, all the way to Cape Carniverous, site of a top-secret missile base. Meanwhile, Rocky and Captain Peachfuzz are getting back to normal, which in the good captain's case means singing the fight song of his alma mater, Waxahachie Normal: *Oh, Waxahachie, fair and proud/ Thy sons and daughters sing out loud/ Our praise for you will never cease/ All hail, the magenta and cerise!*

Two hundred & forty-eight

A blast of goof gas sends America's brightest minds gibbering to the control panel, launching a myriad of missiles all over the map. Luckily, plucky Rocky – alley-ooped by mighty Bullwinkle's moosle-muscled forearm to supersonic, squirrel-fur-singing speed – deflects the missiles in the merest nick of time, sending them crashing down on Pottsylvania, for which brave feat the now-hair-less flying squirrel is made an official astronaut.

BANANA FORMULA

EPISODES 249-260

EVERYONE HAS ONE TALENT,

even if it's just sticking six flashlights in your mouth at once or going over Niagara Falls in a giant bagel, and Bullwinkle's happens to be that he can remember everything he ever ate. Take breakfast, for example, two weeks ago today: six pancakes, four eggs sunny-side up, a slice of ham, three hot dogs, a bowl of chili, and a raisin cookie. Amazing as that is, it's nothing compared to what inventor Bermuda Schwartz has just accomplished across town: He's invented Hushaboom, the first completely silent explosive.

Two hundred & fifty

Inventor Bermuda Schwartz may be a brilliant bomb maker, but he's pretty darn gullible when it comes to his own mother – actually, Boris in

disguise. Once he's conned the gullible professor to hide the Hushaboom formula, Boris adroitly writes it on the inside of a banana peel, then zips said banana back up. Unfortunately, because of his evil nature, Boris can't quite resist selling that very banana to a passing moose for an exorbitant price.

Two hundred & fifty-one

A definitely disgruntled Boris hops a steamroller, intending to commit squash-and-run upon the banana-munching moose, but, just in time, Rocky streaks aloft like a pullet – that is, a bullet – managing to shove Bullwinkle into an open manhole right before the steamroller rumbles past. Repairing to a nearby drugstore (where Boris and Natasha just happen to be hiding under a table) for nerve-soothing sodas, Rocky (and the two villains) realizes that Bullwinkle – whose one talent it is to remember precisely everything he's ever eaten – can regurgitate the formula at will. So to connive the formula out of the gullible moose, Boris dresses up as a giant lollipop and announces that he's Allen Fink, host of the *Candied Camera* TV show; Bullwinkle obliges by gladly telling the banana formula.

Two hundred & fifty-two

Boris manages to get himself arrested as a juvenile delinquent, but presently he's paroled into Natasha's custody. Soon he's pedaling up with a telegram for Moose and Squirrel,

informing them they've won a free weekend at Lake Kitchie Itchie Lodge.

Two hundred & fifty-three

After seventeen hours of straight driving, there's no lake and the lodge is just a big, empty run-down house, so ever-vigilant Rocky is suspicious when strangely familiar Egbert Kitchie Itchie himself arrives, promising to take care of every little thing and showing off the lovely back porch view. Only there is no back porch, and Bullwinkle takes a fast dive into a big bucket of quick-drying cement, which the dastardly Boris quickly breaks open and uses to make a plastic moose mold. Will the fake moose fool Rocky, or did Badenov pick up the wrong dummy?

Two hundred & fifty-four

It is a lovely view, but it goes by so fast, says Bullwinkle after the *second* time he goes flying off the "back porch," which really isn't there at all. Meanwhile, Boris has dolled up his moose mannequin, creating a sexy girl moose who goes by the name of Jane Moosefield, but is actually a walking, talking – *Hello, handsome. Click. This is a recording.* – booby trap designed to snag one

particular antler-headed booby. But Rocky figures out Jane's a dummy, and even though the smitten moose doesn't care how smart she is, he pulls Bullwinkle out of the house – just before Ms. Moosefield blows her top.

Two hundred & fifty-five

Boarding a river steamer for home following the explosion of the lodge, Bullwinkle keeps hiccuping the formula, so Rocky figures what his moose pal needs is a good hiccup doctor – which should be Boris's cue, only the villain has the Pottsylvanian blues and is certain that Moose and Squirrel finally will see through his disguise, so Natasha cheers him with Article Six of the *Villains Handbook*: "There's nobody as stupid as the hero of a TV cartoon show." And lo and behold, when he introduces himself as the ship's doc, our heroes seem more concerned with bad puns (of course they do) than familiar voices and see-through disguises.

Two hundred & fifty-six

Boris and Natasha, with their tape recording of Bullwinkle hiccuping the secret formula, are off to rendezvous with Fearless Leader, jetting in from Pottsylvania. Meanwhile, two terse refugees from *Dragnet* give our heroes a good grilling, clapping the incredulous Bullwinkle ("Official Secrets Act." "*They do?*") into custody before he can spill the

secret formula yet again. And when Rocky calls Army Intelligence a contradiction in terms, the two agents bind and gag him (and the Narrator) too.

Two hundred & fifty-seven

When Fearless Leader listens to the recording and hears Boris calling him ugly, he gets so angry that he knocks himself out shooting at the offending tape recorder. Meanwhile, not only our heroes, but

the Narrator, too, is gagged and bound, but his clipped-cop captors realize their chief can't appear until the customary announcement by the Narrator, along the lines of *and just then a familiar figure entered the room,* so they rip the Narrator's gag – and his moustache – off, enabling Captain Peter "Wrong Way" Peachfuzz to enter the room.

Two hundred & fifty-eight

Peachfuzz frees our heroes, and together, with the aid of the Peter Peachfuzz Polar Path Predictor, patent pending, a powerful electronic direction-divining machine, they set off to find Boris and Natasha, who have just mixed up their first successful batch of Hushaboom.

Two hundred & fifty-nine

As our heroes arrive below, Boris drops a Hushaboom-filled test tube on them, only to remember just barely in time that there's enough explosive in it to blow up the building he and Natasha are in too; so instead, dashing down and snatching the boom tube out of the air, he introduces himself as the world's greatest scientist, J. Robert Oppendowner, and invites Bullwinkle in for a hearty slurp of his latest invention, Soda *Pow*.

Two hundred & sixty

Boris and Natasha take one look at the exploded warehouse and figure Moose and Squirrel are TV cartoon history, but Bullwinkle is feeling fit as a fiddle and twice as stringy after leaving the deadly Soda-*Pow* test tube behind while going off with Rocky to search for a straw to drink it with. A passing sheriff takes one look at Boris and Natasha and arrests them – for spying? for master criminality? for mad-bombing? Not exactly. For being litterbugs, to be precise.

"Hokey Smoke, Bullwinkle!"

BUMBLING BROTHERS CIRCUS

EPISODES 261-270

THE SMALLEST BIG SHOW ON EARTH

has come to Frostbite Falls, and its lion *un*-tamer, Claude Badley, looks suspiciously like Boris Badenov. Yes, rolling into town is the Bumbling Brothers Circus, owned by Hugo and Igo, identical pot-bellied, white-moustached twins in matching ringmaster costumes.

Two hundred & sixty-two

As a lion tamer, Boris is far from lionhearted, using in his act only old and toothless lions of least resistance. But he's got one real roarer ready to set loose, Satan the Maneater... or is that Moose-eater? Or will squirrel turn out to be just what Satan is craving?

Two hundred & sixty-three

Satan the ferociously roaring lion has Rocky trapped under his huge paw, so Bullwinkle tries everything he can think of, including yoo-hooing, flapping a handkerchief and stomping his foot while calling Toro, and doing a tap dance while wearing a funny hat and juggling four balls at a time, but nothing works until he takes out his trusty pocket comb and hums a soothing lullaby. The lion falls directly asleep, and the grateful Bumbling Brothers make Bullwinkle the new lion tamer, firing an outraged Boris on the spot.

Two hundred & sixty-four

Getting fired really burns Boris, so he returns the favor by torching the circus and swiss-cheesing the fire hose, but quick-witted Rocky lines up all the elephants at the water trough and has them shoot trunkfuls of water that extinguish the blaze. Presently, our heroes have new careers: Bullwinkle the musical lion tamer (he puts his head in the lion's mouth and vice versa) and Rocky the elephant trainer. Meanwhile, Boris is looking for something extra special in the *Fireside Book of Fiendish Plans.*

Two hundred & sixty-five

Bullwinkle's got the wild beasts of the circus doing strange and wonderful things, all to the music of his tissue-covered comb, but the circus is going broke anyway because of the constant rain that follows the circus wagons from town to town. So our heroes do the only thing true heroes can do in a perilous and mysterious situation like this: They go out to launch. Bullwinkle alley-oops Rocky straight into the ominous clouds.

Two hundred & sixty-six

ZAP! A zillion-volt bolt of lightning knocks the heroic flying squirrel right into the backseat of a

black 1925 biplane coursing, pilotless, below. Fortunately, the plane lands itself on a mesa, but Rocky is immediately taken prisoner by a tribe of Indians. Meanwhile, Bullwinkle's suspicions are finally aroused when he meets the town mayor, the Right Dishonorable Avaricious J. Wardheeler, but back at the mesa the plucky squirrel is tied to a stake, and the pile of branches on which he's standing is set afire. Now that the network has banned cannibalism, will the network-approved flames finally do our hero in?

Two hundred & sixty-seven

Even the hostile Indians are upset with the network ("All talk, no do," says one dismissively), but that doesn't stop them from trying to give Rocky a full-body hotfoot, until Bullwinkle, who's been chasing Boris through the desert, fortuitously arrives to the rescue. Only the Indians – who are all do and little talk – immediately tie the big moose up too. That's when their leader appears, Big Chief Skunk-Who-Walks-Like-Man, a vaguely familiar menacing figure. The Indians are rain dancers, Rocky explains while the flames flicker nearby, and they've been following the circus and bringing down the rain. Ah-ha! So naturally Bullwinkle whips out his trusty comb and sets the Indians to dancing up a literal storm that douses the fire. But our heroes aren't out of danger yet: When Natasha turns up wearing a Lone Ranger-type hat and mask, Rocky deduces that our heroes must now be villains because the masked rider and his faithful Indian companion are *always* on the side of the law. As if to prove him correct, the Indian archers take dead aim at them. Things really look *arrowing* now.

Two hundred & sixty-eight

Only a sign from the Great Spirit himself can save our heroes from Indian arrows now, and a sign is just what the Badenov-led band gets when an earthquake rattles them. But the quake turns out to be the thundering herd of circus elephants, led by the Bumbling Brothers, to the rescue. With Boris and Natasha hightailing it across the desert, the only problem left is finding room for the Indians, which, as Bullwinkle is happy to inform all and sundry, simply requires making a reservation. Why does Bullwinkle know all the Indian jokes? It's not because he's friends with such famous Indian comedians as Bob Hopi, Red-Skin Skelton, and Phil Silverheels. It's because the moose is part Indian himself, on his Sitting Bullwinkle side.

Two hundred & sixty-nine

Preempted? Maybe. Canceled? Perhaps. But *fired*? Out of the question, after all, Rocky's been doing his usual conscientious job feeding the elephants, and he's been working for peanuts too. Then why are the pachyderms losing so much weight? Could it be that someone's slipping them reducing pills? Could that someone be the water boy, Gunga Drain, who's shown up from another adventure? Nah, 'cause even after Rocky and Bullwinkle get rid of Gunga, the elephants still look downright svelte.

Two hundred & seventy

The reason for the thinning herd is the little boy with the Badenov moustache who's feeding them pep-pill peanuts. But Boris and Natasha have set an even more fiendish trap for Bullwinkle: namely, a poisoned-steel bear trap in the mouth of the fake lion they're in. But just in the nick of time, Rocky shows up with a telegram from fans warning the musical moose not to stick his antlered head into the fake lion's mouth. Soon Boris and Natasha, stuck in the lion suit, have been shipped off to a zoo and the Bumbling Brothers Circus has gone on to great fame, particularly in Great Britain, where it's known as the BBC.

For you who lack horse sense here's...

MR. KNOW-IT-ALL

Hello, racing fans. Today's topic is entitled "How to Do Stunts in the Movies...Without Having the Usher Throw You Out."

You arrive at the studio (Abominable Pictures) and get the first assignment from your (Pottsylvanian-accented) director.

After getting reassurances from your director, you enter a TNT-packed auto and turn the ignition key.

(KA-BOOM!!!!)

War pictures, too, offer a great challenge to the stuntman. After getting reassurances from your director, you dash into a foxhole as all around you bombs go off. After fighting off the foxes, you rescue the dummy there, which turns out to be a bomb, and you realize you're the dummy.

(KA-BOOM!!!!)

Before the day is through, though, you find yourself at the pinnacle of the stuntman's craft, as you find yourself atop a five-thousand foot cliff. After getting reassurances from your director that below you is a fool-

proof safety net, you launch yourself earthward!

The net is there all right...but no one is holding it!

(KER-PLOW!!!)

And so in contusion, to be a stuntman one must always be careful to avoid painful injuries!

MUCHO LOMA MUCH MUD

EPISODES 271–276

SOMEWHERE SOUTH OF THE BORDER

lies the little village of Mucho Loma, or, much mud, whose inhabitants are so weary from sloshing their way through the ever-present mud that they spend much of their time napping to regain their strength. Sometime back, Guadalupe Rodriguez, a singing wayfarer, made his untimely entrance into this town and was promptly clapped into jail for an entire year for disturbing the siesta peace. Released, Guadalupe vows revenge: He outfits himself in a

black mask and black cowboy suit, steals a branding iron with an O on the end, and begins a reign of noisy terror, keeping the weary Mucho Loma citizenry perpetually awake and leaving everywhere the *Brand of Zero!* Meanwhile, our heroes, investigating the level of gas in the tank of their tour bus with a lighter (Bullwinkle's too smart to do it with a match), soon blow into town.

Two hundred & seventy-two

For landing on the town hall and destroying it, our intrepid heroes are sentenced to ninety-nine years, but the judge commutes that to time served on the single condition that they will hunt the dread Zero.

Two hundred & seventy-three

Finding the singing wayfarer's wanted poster on the wall of the Mucho Loma post office is Rocky and Bullwinkle's first clue, and finding Zero himself with his trademark branding iron is their second. Just as they're about to arrest him (the charge isn't jaywalking, Bullwinkle says at one point, it's jay warding), Zero's faithful steed, Esmerelda, bonks them both right into a deep well.

Two hundred & seventy-four

Bullwinkle alley-oops Rocky straight into the sky, and the furry flier throws a line (of the rope variety) to the beleaguered moose. Our heroes then hightail it directly over to Oldberry's Five and Ten, where Rocky buys a complete Zero costume for his moose pal, who, when night falls in Mucho Loma, will be wielding an X-tipped branding iron to trap the night-riding bandit Zero.

Two hundred & seventy-five

Rocket J.'s plan is a masterpiece of steel-trap psychological simplicity: When the noisy desperado appears, Bullwinkle will jump out and the sight of another masked marauder will frighten Zero into leaving the town forever. But there's one small hole in Rocky's plan, and that's the one in the middle of the street that Bullwinkle falls into. By the time he gets back out, Zero hasn't just gotten away, says our Narrator, he's gotten *billscott* clean away, and the angry townsfolk, thinking the costumed moose is Zero, clap Bullwinkle in jail. Now everyone is free to siesta, which puzzles the mighty moose, who's certain 'esta still lives in Frostbite Falls.

Two hundred & seventy-six

The ballad of Mucho Loma lurches to an explosive conclusion when Bullwinkle throws away the stick of TNT disguised as a smelly cigar Rocky gave him. The TNT blows over a brick chimney, which lands on an awning, which catapults the bricks across the street and through a window, which shatters; and the shattered pieces of sharp glass sever a nearby telephone pole, which collapses, smashing the jailhouse wall and freeing Bullwinkle. Still, there's the little matter of the masked marauder, Zero, which Rocky concludes with a triumphant game of tic-tac-toe, using the X- and O- tipped branding irons: When it's Zero's chance to win, the bandit can't resist leaping out of hiding to apply his mark. But in the end, the singing bandit is paroled to work the scoreboard at Yankee Stadium, while our heroes won't be having a new adventure for thirty days.

POTTSYLVANIA CREEPER

EPISODES 277–282

THE BIG NEWS IN TOWN

is the annual Frostbite Falls Flower Fair and Plant Pageant, so our heroes mosey (or is that "moosey"?) on down the Old Ox Road to enter Rocky's Checkered Begonia in the competition, when none other than the world's greatest seed seller, Pete McMoss, and his Pottsylvanian assistant, Ivy C. Halls (the "C" stands for "covered," dollink) sell them a special bean seed, directly descended from the one that grew into Jack's magic beanstalk.

Two hundred & seventy-eight

The Frostbite Falls high school gym is a lovely site for the Flower Fair and Plant Pageant, even though a basketball game has been misscheduled for the same time as the fair and the ball players are slam-dunking casaba melons. Nonetheless, Bullwinkle's quick-grow plant wins first place all right, but it's a rather toothy winner, which proceeds to gulp down not only the judge, but a passing cop as well.

Two hundred & seventy-nine

Bullwinkle's blue-ribbon winner just keeps getting bigger and bigger, and its smile just keeps getting toothier and toothier, and what's more, it won't even stay rooted to one spot. What could it be? A passing federal plant inspector, J. Edgar Bloomer by name, informs our heroes that what they have is the only known example of the dread, vicious, man-eating plant,  the Pottsylvania creeper, which gulps down the F.P.I. man and still has its tendrils set for a nice squirrel snack.

Two hundred & eighty

Seeing Squirrel gulped down by a giant man-eating plant is too momentous a moment for Boris and Natasha alone, so Fearless Leader arrives for the big scene. But Bullwinkle won't let his furry friend down without a flight…directly back to their house and straight under the bed! Is Moose turning chicken? Not at all, he's just scrambling around under there for a hand blowtorch with which to burn the creeper's far-flung roots. While the chlorophyll hotfoot works well enough so that Rocket J. Squirrel can soar out of the plant's deadly grasp, the creeper soon grows a thorny defense and appears about to devour the entire town of Frostbite Falls.

Two hundred & eighty-one

Vegetable Bites Man – now, that's national news! In fact, a White House cabinet meeting has already determined that dealing with the creeper is not a job for the Defense Department because, whatever the leafy menace may be, it's clearly not a defense plant. But the creeper is launching thousands of parachuting seeds, while Rocky is launching himself against the creeper, but that sharpshooting villain, Fearless Leader, has the fearless squirrel right in his sights.

Two hundred & eighty-two

A near miss by Fearless Leader has Rocky stunned and falling, but Bullwinkle, who's run home and gotten his catcher's mitt, snags the squirrel just before the final out. Nonetheless, the creeper's seeds have had just enough time to disperse all over the country, and nothing works against the inexorable munching and growing blight, until Rocky realizes they've tried everything except being nice. It works! The Pottsylvanian creeper can deal viciously with any adversity, but do-gooding gives the giant plant the sudden shrivels, and soon the menace is leafy history, except for the one tiny seed that floats out over the ocean and drops into the submarine in which the baddies are commuting back to Pottsylvania. *Burp!* Meanwhile, back in again-peaceful Frostbite Falls, Bullwinkle is returning with an armload of plant and flower books that he just checked out from – where else? – the *branch* library.

MOOSYLVANIA

EPISODES 283–286

LOOKING AS ALWAYS FOR SOMETHING

Two hundred & eighty-four

Bullwinkle opens the wrong volume, so when there's no bang from the book, Boris rushes in and heedlessly opens the booby-trapped volume himself, but just before the *BLAM!,* Rocky and Bullwinkle are moved by tiny Moosylvania's many narrow flashback misses at becoming an American state (the Betsy Ross Flag Company, for example, wanted to charge extra when George Washington proposed to add Moosylvania to the thirteen colonies. That made it the first casualty of the government's battle against deficit spending), and they head off to Washington to rectify matters Moosylvanian, but Boris has another dastardly trick up his sleeve: He's disguised Butte, Montana, to look like Washington, D.C.!

Two hundred & eighty-five

Why is Boris so intent on foiling our heroes' plan to go to Washington, D.C., and file for Moosylvanian statehood? Because he thinks then he'd lose the distribution rights to evil, that's why. And why are our heroes so intent on making Moosylvania a state? To set an example for Texas, that's why. But no sooner do they disembark their train in the Boris-disguised Butte, where the Capitol dome is topped with a green statue of Frankenstein, than the thirteen-thousand-ton beaverboard mock-up comes crashing down on their heads.

Two hundred & eighty-six

When the fake Capitol falls, Rocky and Bullwinkle nimbly dodge the crash, but the shock wave sets off a chain reaction and all the Boris-built false fronts fall, but then the Butte, Montana, buildings behind *them* fall too, revealing…the *real*

BULLWINKLE RECOMMENDS LOCAL CLEANERS

to help others get a little more pain out of life, Boris and Natasha devise a most fiendish contest: *I like being evil because…*, in twenty-five words or less, sweeps the country, and when Bullwinkle J. Moose enters under the mistaken impression that it's a why-I-like-*weevils* contest, his answer – that he had distribution rights on 'em in Moosylvania for two years and almost made a fortune – immediately wins first prize, which just happens to be the deluxe edition of the *Encyclopedia Badenov,* which just happens to contain a very explosive entry under "Moosylvania."

Washington, D.C., which had been cleverly rigged to look like Butte, Montana, by a pressure group in the pay of the Montana Muskmellon Trust. But decorating the entire town doesn't sway our legislators, who proudly vote against Medicare even though the reformers stick fifty-four million bandages on the Washington Monument! Meanwhile, Boris convinces the trusting Moose and Squirrel to hand him the statehood-for-Moosylvania petition, but instead the absent-minded moose hands the Pottsylvanian villain the gift he's just been given by the New Mexico Dynamite and TNT Trust, a *really* high-pressure group. So statehood for Moosylvania is an explosive issue after all!

RUBY YACHT

EPISODES 287-292

ON THE SANDY SHORES OF

Veronica Lake, Bullwinkle launches his special sailing vessel, a dusty toy dhow – that is, a traditional sailing vessel used primarily in the Indian Ocean and the Red Sea – in the annual Frostbite Falls Flotilla Festival, but the hapless vessel promptly sinks (which is good enough for a first-prize ribbon in the submarine category anyway). After the little boat is retrieved, it shines like new, twinkling with a rich ruby glow. If it's made from rubies, that can mean only one thing…Bullwinkle has come into possession of…the *Ruby Yacht* of Omar Khayyam!

Two hundred & eighty-eight

Bullwinkle says he wants to sail the *Ruby Yacht* at an interesting party, but the press, as usual, gets it wrong, and before long, halfway round the world, in the northern section of Lower East Pakistan, an exotic ruler (no, not the measuring kind) of a remote city peruses with interest a newspaper ad that reads *Moose Will Sell Ruby Yacht of Omar Khayyam to Any Interested Party* and orders his grand vizier to cross the Great Desert separating Lower East Pakistan from Central Minnesota to do a deal for that dhow. But when Bullwinkle refuses the turbaned emissary's final offer, twenty scimitar-wielding soldiers appear.

Two hundred & eighty-nine

The esteemed pasha of a certain remote city will be a very esteemed *off* pasha if his grand vizier doesn't prize the prize *Ruby Yacht* from a certain Minnesota moose, but even though he's been lavished with four Roger Maris baseball cards and a warped long-playing record of tenor Jan Peerce singing "Bluebirds of Happiness," Bullwinkle will not budge, so the grand vizier kidnaps our heroes, intending to make good his escape despite the eagle eyes of watchful customs officials, by disguising Rocky, Bullwinkle, himself, and his men as the ship's orchestra on the S.S. *Plankton,* even now leaving port.

Two hundred & ninety

Guy Vizier and His Tremulous Troubadours don't exactly produce toe-tapping harmonies, but Rocky takes advantage of his bass solo to attach a hacksaw to his bow and cut his chains. Soon he and Bullwinkle are hiding in a lifeboat that just happens to get thrown over the side into a rising sea.

Two hundred & ninety-one

Bullwinkle and Rocky row for all they're worth in the direction of New York, but unbeknownst to them the lifeboat is snagged by one of the S.S. *Plankton*'s mooring cables, and two weeks later they arrive in…Bombay, from which the vizier immediately transports them to the remote city of Jaipur, where the merciless pasha demands return of the sacred *Ruby Yacht* to the sacred shrine, actually a very nice bathtub. When Bullwinkle doesn't instantly comply, he's taken to the very edge of the cobra pit, where the vizier promises to teach him the "error of false pride," something another leading man was threatened with, as the fearless cineaste moose points out, in *Gunga Din.*

Two hundred & ninety-two

Rocky demands prudence of the juris kind, so they adjourn from the cobra pit to the courtroom, where the Rocket gets them off with some fancy ship–model building, and in return Bullwinkle promises to enter no contests again until the Frostbite Falls Marble Shootout, when, the sportsmoose assures Rocky, he will restrict himself to his oblong aggie with the word "hope" on its side. A gem of a reference, doncha think?

BULL'S TESTIMONIAL DINNER

EPISODES 293-298

IT'S A SKYSCRAPER OF

a tall story this time when our heroes hit the high road to Shanghai. Why? Because of his faithful service as a snowplow with antlers, the grateful citizens of Frostbite Falls, Minnesota – having weathered another winter – are toasting Bullwinkle at a testimonial dinner, but, unfortunately, the spot on his best dress shirt has a disconcerting inclination to spread. Need we say more?

Two hundred & ninety-four

Arriving on the fast plane to Shanghai, our heroes hike directly over to the corner of Main and Chow, where they "spot" Ed Foo Yung's Chinese laundry, and Boris and Natasha too.

Two hundred & ninety-five

Yes, the two spies have used their position at a local toy company to develop a miniature atom bomb wristwatch. However will they smuggle it back into the States? A shirt at the laundry, of course, one that turns out to belong to a certain Moose.

Two hundred & ninety-six

Rocky and Bullwinkle have the shirt, but in their flight they've stumbled into the notorious Shanghai waterfront, and they're going to get taken to the cleaners, at the very least, if Boris and Natasha discover them in the hold of the junk they're piloting.

Two hundred & ninety-seven

The junk obviously came from a junkyard, because no sooner has it set off down the river than it lists to port, then to muscatel, then splits open and sinks. Ashore, Bullwinkle is captured by Boris and his henchmen. Meanwhile, time is about to run out on Bullwinkle's atomic shirt.

Two hundred & ninety-eight

Bullwinkle won't tell where he's hidden the shirt with the atomic bomb – it's the dean of the thing, he says, or at least the principal. That's when Boris resorts to torture, forcing the peckish moose to watch Natasha eat a scrumptious banana split. Understandably, Bullwinkle cracks and reveals he's sitting on it. The bad guys split with their ill-gotten miniature bomb, which immediately blows up, raining litter down on Shanghai (after all, it's only a cartoon atomic bomb). As for our heroes, they make it back to Frostbite Fall just in time for Bullwinkle to appear at his testimonial dinner wearing a tie, tails, and a snazzy flashing-neon pizza-parlor sign instead of a stuffy old formal shirt.

"There's a little bad in everything good that happens."

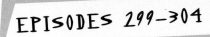

THE WEATHER LADY

IT'S THE END OF

unpredictable weather in Frostbite Falls, for the Committee for Civic Improvement has scraped together thirty-three dollars and fifteen cents and purchased a fortune-telling machine from an abandoned penny arcade: Put a coin in the slot, the lady in the window deals a hand of cards and the hand forecasts the weather. Card-playing ability like that catches Boris's and Natasha's attention, and before you can say "Fiendish Plan," the blond weather lady's been purloined. But the keen-visaged squirrel notices tire tracks leading from the scene of the crime and he and his faithful moose companion take off in hot pursuit.

Three hundred

The tracks lead to an empty van in the middle of a very loudly creaking bridge with an understructure sawed almost all the way through by you-know-who, who watches the big bridge collapse from the top of nearby Sam Hill. Some fancy last-second stepping averts disaster for our heroes, but by this time Boris and Natasha have reached the near-by river town of Watchowee Falls, where, before you can say "four-of-a-kind," they use the weather lady to win a steamboat from a local shipbuilder by the name of Hiram Trump.

Three hundred & one

Hearing about the fabulous poker lady cleaning up at the gambling riverboat that Boris has rechristened the *Sands Hotel,* Rocky deduces that she and the missing weather lady are one and the same. So Bullwinkle, masquerading as a southern colonel, comes aboard to play the lucky poker lady. Meanwhile, Rocky surreptitiously short-circuits the lights so Bullwinkle can snatch the card-playing, fortune-telling weather lady in the ensuing darkness, or, anyway, that's the plan. But Boris has a plan of his own: to turn Moose's lights off permanently.

Three hundred & two

Natasha fires an elephant gun at the exact instant Rocky plunges the riverboat into darkness. In the ensuing confusion Bullwinkle makes the snatch, but back ashore, our heroes realize that the speedy but erroneous moose has come away with a phone booth, so naturally they use it to call Boris, who cannot resist when Rocky offers the magnificent sum of fifty smackers in trade for the purloined weather lady.

Three hundred & three

In the middle of Main Street, they meet to trade, but when the vigilant moose spots a buzzing mosquito on Boris's cheek and swats it, the townsfolk naturally assume that a southern gentleman like Colonel Bullwinkle intends to meet Boris at dawn for a duel, while the moose himself is under the impression that "a duel" means "good-bye" in French. However, the day turns out to be so beautiful that everyone decides to have a picnic instead of a gunfight, and later Rocky and Boris go ahead with the trade. But the dastardly Boris reneges and leaves Rocky and Bullwinkle with only three ninety-eight to their names. Fortunately, the Dingaling Brothers Circus arrives in town and it just so happens that it needs a high platform diver, so, by giving three performances a day, the plucky squirrel raises over a thousand dollars by the time the circus moves on, and you can be sure he intends to bet the whole amount – all eleven hundred dollars and fifteen cents – against the unbeatable weather lady.

Three hundred & four

Rocky issues his challenge and Bullwinkle arrives aboard the riverboat with…another fortune-telling machine! Like hard boiled eggs, the four kings Bullwinkle's machine comes up with will be hard to beat, but the weather lady extracts for her deck… *four aces,* then, just as Rocky expected, she suddenly overheats. In the confusion and darkness, Boris and Natasha try to escape with both machines in a rowboat, but the overloaded little vessel promptly sinks. Sometime later, back in Frostbite Falls, none other that those two civic-minded TV heroes, Rocky and Bullwinkle, are doing their civic duty in matching fortune-telling machines.

LOUSE ON NINETY-SECOND STREET

EPISODES 305–310

WE CAN'T ALL BE HEROES,

but it's perfectly acceptable to *have* a hero. Rocky's, of course, is Bullwinkle, and so is Bullwinkle's. Even Boris has a hero; namely, Fingers Scarnose, who was born to a life of crime in Heck's Kitchen, just below the Lower East Side. As a four-year-old, he stole a diaper truck, but of course they couldn't pin it on him, and he even graduated *magna cum lousy* from reform school. But in his long criminal career, he's never been convicted in court, because no witness is brave enough to testify against him.

Three hundred & six

In the midst of his onion shopping, Bullwinkle happens to pass by the bank that Scarnose is holding up. Mistaking the getaway car for a taxi, Bullwinkle jumps in just before the getaway-minded Scarnose gang does. Will Scarnose and his thugs realize that there's a moose in on the vamoose, and that he just might be the very witless – that is, wit*ness* – everyone's looking for?

Three hundred & seven

Scarnose finally notices the moose with the bag of bermudas sitting in the getaway car, but just then the bullets start flying and the onions get blown to eye-watering bits, which makes the teary driver spin out of control, throwing Bullwinkle to the pavement. But will the moose live long enough to sing Scarnose into Sing Sing?

Three hundred & eight

It's Bullwinkle's dangerous duty to testify against crime lord Fingers Scarnose, but Scarnose intends to torpedo that, so he employs an out-of-town torpedo – none other than Boris Badenov – to do in the dutiful moose before he can do his civic duty. It isn't long before a sweet little old lady with a Pottsylvanian accent turns up at Bullwinkle's door selling an apple with a fuse sizzling out of it.

Three hundred & nine

As Boris and Natasha take cover, Rocky discovers that the worm in the apple is actually a burning fuse, so the plucky squirrel plucks the bomb from the horrified moose, flies it out the window, and

drops it right into a certain garbage can, where a certain pair of distinctly unlucky villains are hiding. Speaking of hiding, that's just what our heroes do, going undercover at a mink farm until the day Bullwinkle has to testify, which is just when Boris turns up. So at Rocky's urgent urging, the mighty moose dives into the mink pen and gives it his best minkish mime.

Three hundred & ten

When Rocky returns to the mink pen after taking cover for two hours, he discovers that a certain foreign gentleman has purchased the biggest mink on the farm – who didn't go willingly. Taking to the air, Rocky discovers that the mink-tied moose is about to lose his own fur coat to a sawmill's toothy buzz, while Boris and Natasha eagerly await, so the quick-witted squirrel dives into an abandoned office and telephones the electric company, saying that the sawmill can't pay its utility bill. Naturally, all the power is instantly shut off. While Boris and Natasha go off to check the fuse box, Rocky frees Bullwinkle and they race to make it back to the courthouse in time to testify. At the very last instant, the mooseness – that is, *wit*ness – appears and his detailed testimony – "he did it!" – sends Scarnose to the slammer.

WOSSAMOTTA U

EPISODES 311→322

AT A LARGE MINNESOTA COLLEGE,

the answer to the question Wossamotta U is… *everything;* yes, Wossamotta University has lost eighty percent of its enrollment and its buildings are crumpling, all because there's no winning football team! What's Wossamotta U to do? Fire a few English teachers, for starters, to get the best football talent scouts money can buy, who, soon thereafter, accidentally wander into Frostbite Falls just as Bullwinkle J. Moose gives Rocket J. Squirrel an emergency alley-oop into town to get a missing ingredient for his salami soufflé. And before you can say Jack Robins, the speedy squirrel shoots into town, buys his powder, and

speeds back. And so before you can say Jack Ro – the talent scouts sign our heroes to a college football scholarship.

Three hundred & twelve

The moose matriculates, but since he's on a football scholarship, the only classic the Frostbite Falls Flash has to study is *Dick and Jane at the Seashore.* But when it comes time to suit up and fire a pass, Bullwinkle can't find cleats for his size twenty-twos or his throwing arm.

Three hundred & thirteen

Coach Canute is amazed when Rocky shows him the alley-oop pass, and the amazed college trustees immediately start building their big new stadium in anticipation of great new victories, like the bug upset over Watchmakers College – or as it's known, Tick Tock Tech – or the unusual victory over Barely Normal. Pretty soon, though, Boris sees big bucks in fixing a game and betting on the rigged result.

Three hundred & fourteen

Moose can throw passes, but can he throw an entire game? wonders Boris, himself not a graduate of Penn State but of the state pen, so he enlists Natasha to feign distress – dis dress, dat dress, all she knows is she's distraught – so she plays on good-hearted Bullwinkle's sympathy by telling him her brother is on the Hard Knocks school team, and that if Hard Knocks doesn't win on Saturday, he'll be thrown off and lose his letter sweater – and, gee, it's turning cold too.

WOSSAMOTTA U.
USES THE NOODLE 1952 GOOD'S SMARTUS

Wossamotta U. hereby confers the title of
Wagner Cum Laude, Artypay Artyhay, Toto Otnay Inhay Ansaskay
on _____
(Your Name Here!)
In recognition of extraordinary Fun, Silliness, Humor, and _____
Date _____   President _____

Three hundred & fifteen

Bullwinkle *sell out*? Well, heroes *are* supposed to help damsels in distress, aren't they? Comes the big game against Hard Knocks College, and the odds on Wossamotta are long, but so are Natasha Fatale's batty eyelashes, and when Boris impersonates her brother too, good-hearted Bullwinkle is completely taken in, until the big game's last quarter, when he spots Natasha and Boris in the stands, cheering for Hard Knocks. Then, in his eagerness to get at the fiendish Boris, the adamant moose runs right for the wrong goal! Will it be a fool's goal, and is defeat staring our heroes in the face?

Three hundred & sixteen

Right at the edge of the wrong goal line, with a horde of tacklers in pursuit, the furious moose stops, spots Boris, who's beat a hasty retreat to the other side of the field, and throws the first handy object at the fleeing villain, namely, the football. Just as the speeding forward pass reaches the end zone, Rocky zooms up, snagging it for the winning points, and Wossamotta becomes the top team in the country, but those two heels without souls, Boris and Natasha, can't just walk away. They have a new Fiendish Plan in mind: Assemble their own football team, the Mud City Manglers, with the toughest thugs in the state, coached by that homicidal martinet, Fearless Leader, who's back for a – *POW!* – guest shot.

Three hundred & seventeen

Boris hits on a novel way to up the odds on the Mud City Manglers: He dresses the brawny goons and criminals up in mini-blouses and curly wigs, promoting them as a girls team. *Debutantes to Tackle Wossamotta Juggernaut* the headlines scream. Will these male bags disguised as dolls deliver the knockout punch to mighty Wossamotta, or will it be another red-letter game day?

Three hundred & eighteen

The odds on the Big Conflict?…World War III? – six to five and pick'em. Wossamotta versus a girls team? – five hundred to one, so naturally Boris and Fearless Leader bet the entire Pottsylvanian treasury on Mud City, and naturally, to protect their little bet, the Fiendish Plan needs a Fiendish Plan of its own; namely, kidnap Bob Waterbucket, the Wossamotta quarterback. But when Bullwinkle is drafted to take over, he's ready, after a fashion, because for three weeks he's been studying old Civil War battles instead of his playbook.

Three hundred & nineteen

The Mud City Manglers have an unconventional defensive strategy, which includes digging trenches and setting up a gun emplacement, for the first half of the big game against the Wossamotta Pigeons. But since the Manglers are using battle tactics anyway, the battle plans Bullwinkle's been studying up on work out just fine in the second half.

Three hundred & twenty

Colonel moose takes those Civil War battle plans rather seriously, running north despite the fact that the Wossamotta goal lines are to the south, and, to make certain that the wrong side wins, a Mud City Mangler keeps a gun pointed right at the referee's fifty-yard line. All over the country bookmakers are taking three-to-one that they'll never make another bet again, all because mighty Wossamotta is taking a pounding from Mud City.

Three hundred & twenty-one

When a Mud City Mangler is caught intimidating the ref, Bullwinkle springs into action, replaying the final two years of the Civil War in the last ten minutes of gridiron action, and just before the final gun sounds, the speedy squirrel zooms for the goal line, but just at that moment Boris hurls a large rock at the diminutive Rocky.

Three hundred & twenty-two

Hokey smoke! Rocky dodges, the referee ducks, and the rock bonks the Mud City thug holding a gun to the ref's back. Mud City mounts an all-out assault, but out of the pall of smoke and flame covering the gridiron comes galloping none other than Bullwinkle J. Moose, the football dangling from an antler, and even though Boris has taken the precaution of mining the entire Wossamotta end zone, swivel-hips Bullwinkle crosses all the way through without a toe touching a single explosive. But when Boris puts a questioning tootsie in the end zone's vicinity…*KA-BOOM!*

MOOSYLVANIA SAVED

EPISODES 323–326

FEARLESS LEADER DOESN'T LIKE

hearing bad news unless he's thought of it first himself, and this the worst: The Pottsylvanian national treasury is broke! But Fearless has a Fiendish Plan, and soon Boris will find himself in the wettest, soggiest, dreariest place on earth – Moosylvania, of course, the only country that has the distinction of being fought over by both the United States and Canada, with each country insisting it belongs to the other – where even now Rocky and Bullwinkle are vacationing.

Three hundred & twenty-four

Moosylvania's a magnificent catastrophe all right, and it's been in the Bullwinkle family for years, so naturally the vaguely familiar-looking head of Dancer, Prancer, Blitzen, & Fink, the largest advertising agency in all of North America, wants to help make it the riviera of the swamps! But Boris actually has a better idea: He sinks Rocky and Bullwinkle's boat, marooning them in Moosylvania, then sends word that the two heroes are in need. Quickly, a grateful nation springs into action, airlifting tons and tons of such badly needed supplies as two thousand gallons of maple syrup, eight hundred surplus goldfish bowls, twenty-six obsolete missiles, twenty-two gross of emergency collar buttons, forty-six tons of bubble gum, and a coupon from Dr. Kildare good for one emergency appendectomy. As the emergency foreign aid piles up, the isle of Moosylvania begins to sink.

Three hundred & twenty-five

Boris and Natasha are stealing as fast as they can, but Moosylvania is going down even faster,

and Bullwinkle J. Moose, hereditary governor of Moosylvania and a determined sinker (or words to that effect) is planning to go down with his state. Does Bullwinkle have one last request? A nice piece of gum, and with that, a bright idea bubbles up in Rocky's brain: Throwing boxes of bubble gum into a handy nearby cement mixer, the brainy squirrel zooms over to a large tank of surplus helium, fastens a hose to the batch of bubble-making goo, and, quicker that you can say *SPLAT!*, the speedy squirrel is tying large helium-filled gum balloons to the island, which stops sinking and slowly reemerges from the swamp. Good loser that he is, Boris lights a stick of dynamite and hurls it toward our heroes.

Three hundred & twenty-six

If that TNT goes off, the gooey balloons will go bust and the foreign-aid–laden little island of Moosylvania will go down for the count beneath the swampy waves, so naturally Boris dashes after it, throwing it down into a funny-looking trash barrel that, an exasperated Natasha informs him, is the ventilator on their submarine. Shortly thereafter, a friendly neighborhood moving man, one Van N. Storridge, appears, offering to move all that unsightly foreign aid for our two trusting heroes, and before long, Boris is on a supply-laden barge that rendezvous with Fearless Leader's submarine in mid-ocean, where a grateful Fearless gives a beaming Boris the Pottsylvanian Double Cross Medal, which just happens to weigh exactly enough so that its addition sinks the enormous barge. Could this be the end, our gone-fishin' heroes want to know, or does it just seem like it's going to be a long time until the next episode?

And now here's that master of the cinematic arts...

Cinematic arts, nuthin'!
This is about the movies!
Today our subject is "How to Direct Temperamental Movie Stars."
And our first example is a child star (with a familiar moustache)… little Muriel Merkle. I am the only director in Hollywood who can make Muriel laugh. First, I don my Confederate costume: Awright Muriel, the colonel has come home from the war. Let's have a big laugh.
A nice big laugh for America, Muriel: Watch Uncle Bullwinkle hit himself over the head!

(TH-WAAP!!! HA-HA-HA-HA!!!)

Next we have Hoot Mix, a real (Pottsylvanian-accented) he-man who never lets a stunt man do any of his hard scenes. Okay, Hoot, let's see you fight with the dummy.

(KA-BOOM!!! SMASH-SMASH-SMASH!!!)

Hey, ouch! That wasn't in the script! Quit ad-libbing!
Next, we have handsome (oddly-moustached) Dick Farnsworth, the moet temperamental man in the industry! But I am so good I have even persuaded him to do a soap commercial. Really:

ACTION!

Okay, Zippy: What is it you do with the soap of Hollywood stars?

(BONG!!!)

(GULP!)

So here's a final tip–

(HICCUP!)

Never *eat* the soap of Hollywood Stars!

(HIC!)

ALL ON THiS
iTTY-BiTTY
CARD

Like the veteran performers and vaudevillians that they are, Rocky and Bullwinkle are never at a loss for words... many of which—three-and-a-half decades after the debut of their TV show—still remain part of the hip lexicon. Words and phrases and bits of business like these: And now here's something we hope you'll really like!

Newt descending a staircase.

Hello there, culture gang!

One nation in dirigible.

Bullwinkle was also an MIT graduate, that is of course,

the Moose Institute of Toe Dancing. The Cedar Yorpantz Flying School was Rocky's alma mater.

"Bacon, you'll fry for this!" rants Shakespeare after being beaned on the noggin by an irate Francis Bacon in a "Fractured Fairy Tale."

I was cuke as a coolcumber.

(i.e. Tick Tock Tech Watchmaker Technical Institute, which was Wossamotta U's opponent in the Big Game)

"For a powerful magnate, you sure don't pick up things too quickly," sez Rocky to a dimbulb shipping tycoon.

Bullwinkle is a dope!

"Sure is dark in here," sez Rocky.

All on this itty-bitty card.

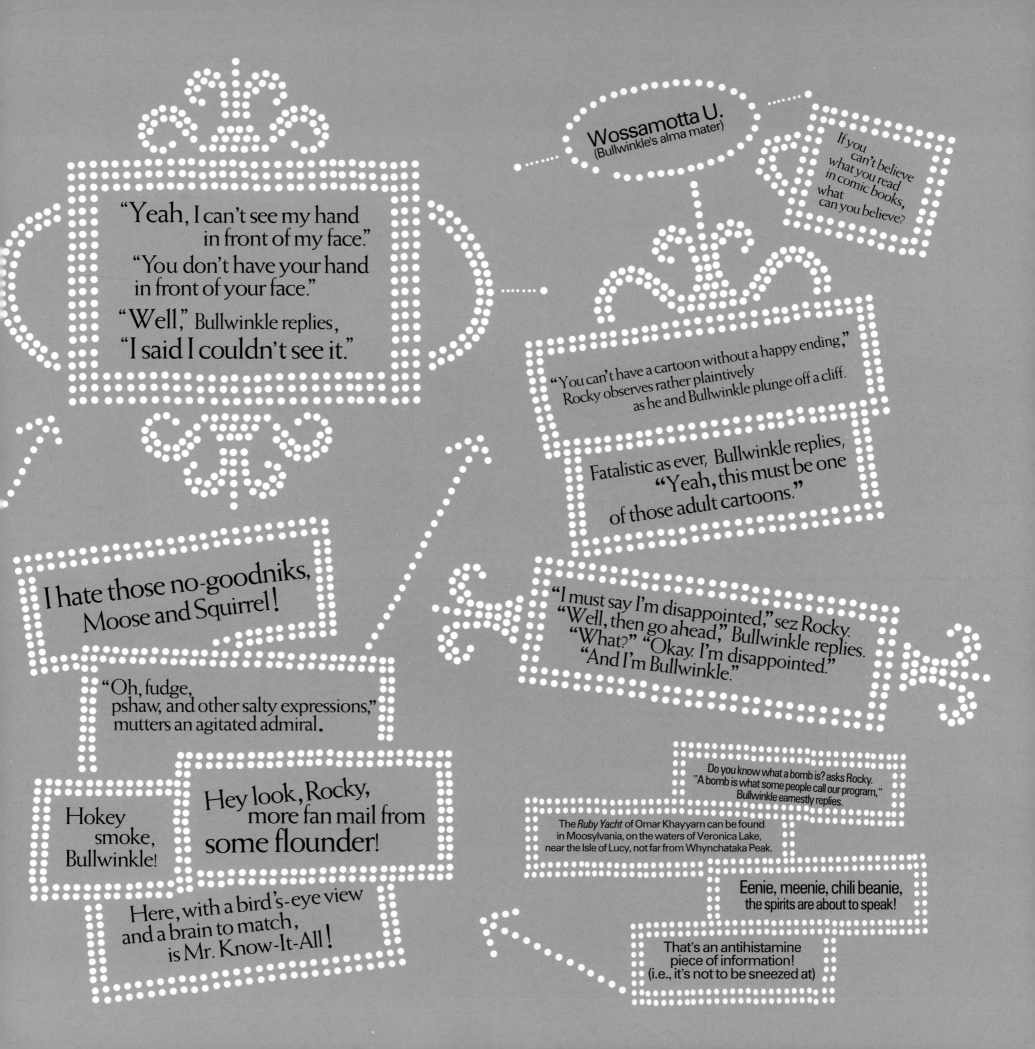

"Boris, dahlink, throw the medal overboard!"

"But – Fearless Leader heemself gave that to me!"

"Badenov! You're seen-king the whole cargo!"

"Vot happens if eet sinks?"

"You get shot!"

"Vot happens if I throw a-vay dee medal?"

"You get shot!"

"Vell – at least I gotta choice. Now let me see..."

"Well, the ol' place is back to subnormal, Rock."

"Yeah, and we–"

  BANG!

"Hey, was that a shot?"

"Heck no, Rock."

"Well, it sounded like a shot."

"Nope."

"Then what was it?"

"That was... The End."

"By George, he's got it! It is the end. But watch for

  another episode soon of...ROCKY AND BULLWINKLE!"

"It may be a little hard to find, but don't give up."

"We're not."

The Romaine Street Savoyards – as Jay Ward, with piping-voiced irony, called the little troupe of expert voice actors who'd been meeting for more than three-and-a-half years, usually weekly, usually in the afternoons and evenings, at the sound recording studio on Romaine Street in Hollywood, to record what was then called *The Bullwinkle Show* – gather for the last time on a cool and hazy December afternoon in 1962. The dapper Paul Frees (Boris), the peripatetic Bill Scott (Bullwinkle), tiny June Foray (both Rocket J. Squirrel and Natasha Fatale), and William Conrad (the breathless narrator) are at their customary spots by the microphones. As usual, Jay Ward is in the control booth.

They take it from the top, racing through the dialogue at the usual velocity: warped speed. *"And so it was a short time later that a makeshift barge loaded with a fantastic amount of surplus goodies headed out to the open sea,"* but Conrad comes in with his lines a mere beat late. The Savoyards fairly screech to a halt.

"So, I'm late," says the actor airily.

"Not only late, but lousy," cracks Frees. Even before the show, they'd been friends for years.

Conrad harrumphs, appealing to the court of highest authority: "You can't be great on alla them, right, Jay baby?"

From the booth the director silently signals another take.

"It's a lucky thing directors don't have to talk," Conrad continues, as usual trying to get a rise out of the extravagantly moustachioed man behind the glass. *"And so it was a short time later that –"* He fumbles the line again.

"Oh, no," exclaims June Foray with mock horror, breaking into a throaty laugh. For three hundred and twenty-six episodes these guys have been breaking her up – particularly Conrad, who, with obvious affection, likes to tease her, calling her "a poor little drunken girl" whenever she trips over a word, and Scott, who regularly startles her with sudden *SCREECH*ings and other sound effects.

From the booth comes Ward: "Looks like a long evening after all, folks," he says brightly, but they get it on the third take, racing through to that final good-bye.

"Aw," says Conrad, after the last line, "that's sad."

"Yeah," agrees June in her Rocky voice, the chirpiness gone suddenly melancholy.

Scott gallumps Bullwinkle-like, "Aw, I don't wanna. I don't wanna." And then the actors go out into the night, and Rocky and Bullwinkle go into TV history.

THE END

(I don't wanna, I don't wanna)

TWO FINAL WORDS
FROM THE AUTHOR

GENTLE READER:

Writing may be magic, but there are some rabbits that not even a mighty Minnesota moose can pull out of the hat, and getting the entirety of the Rocky and Bullwinkle oeuvre between the covers of a single book is certainly one of them. So to you Far-Flung Frostbite Falls Flyers and Moosylvanians Manqué everywhere, who had hoped, perhaps, for learned exegesis of the semiotic significance of, say, the fairy tales and more than just brief guest appearances by the distinguished likes of Dudley and Peabody, I have just two words:

Im-possible!

But fret not. Stay tuned until our next episode....

Hollywood, California, and Frostbite Falls, Minnesota

May 1996